Miracles

God's Heavenly Touch On Man

Gary L. Wood

MIRACLES

ISBN-13: 978-0-9892213-8-2

ISBN-10: 0-9892213-8-5

Library of Congress Control Number: 2013956362

Printed in the United States of America.

RevMedia Publishing
PO Box 5172
Kingwood, TX 77325

A publishing division of Revelation Ministries

www.revmediapublishing.com

Dedication

This book is dedicated to my precious wife Deena who has stood beside me for the past 40 years as a faithful friend and companion. And also to my two precious children, Angel and David, who are both miracles and such a joy and blessing to us. A special love is sent to my mother and father-in-law who have literally accepted me as their son.

Acknowledgments

Many thanks to Steve and Mary Vanides whom God miraculously led into our lives and making this book possible.

A special thanks to Nancy Holland and the editorial staff, and to Rich Kreegier for the cover design.

Above all to the King of Kings and Greatest Miracle Worker Who continues to touch our lives every day... Thank You, Jesus!

Table of Contents

Who Is Jesus?

He never wrote a book and yet there are more books written about Him than any other man.

He never wrote a song, yet there are more songs about Him than any other person.

He never outlined a sermon, yet He has more masterpieces and more sermons than any other preacher.

He never attended a college, yet He has more students studying His laws than any other university.

He never marshaled an army, yet there are more soldiers that would fight for Him than any general that ever marched an army.

He never practiced medicine, yet one mouthful of spit upon the dumb man's tongue has more healing remedy than all the physicians' medicine in the world.

He never held an office; never established a budget;

Never designed a letterhead; never built a church building; He left with no fanfare, gave no date for

His return, yet more people are looking for Him to come back than any other man.

What Child Is This?

Some say He was just a good teacher, but good teachers don't claim to be God.

Some say He was merely a good example, but good examples don't mingle with prostitutes and sinners.

Some say He was a madman, but madmen don't speak the way He spoke.

Some say He was a crazed lunatic, but crazed lunatics don't draw children to themselves or attract men of intellect like Paul or Luke to be their followers.

Some say He was a religious phony, but phonies don't rise from the dead.

Some say He was a ghost, but ghosts can't give their flesh and blood to be crucified.

Some say He was a myth, but myths don't set the calendar for history. Jesus was the ideal man. He was an example of love and the greatest teacher who ever lived.

He is my Lord and Savior and that's what Christianity is all about.

INTRODUCTION

A WORD FROM GOD

That which I have deposited with you, saith God, I will bring to the time of fulfillment. I have written it on the tablets of your heart and you have leaned anxiously to wait to see it in manifestation. I say to you that the day is before you to proclaim and speak forth My Word and stand fast in that which I have planted within you. It shall come forth out of you even as I promised for I have not forsaken you. I have not forgotten you nor the call I have placed on you, saith the Lord of Hosts.

Prophecy Given to Gary Wood:

For the Lord would say unto you, Gary and Deena, yea even though it has been difficult at times for you to be where I called you to be and even though you had to fight battle after battle to attain the goals you set at My direction, you have been faithful. Your faithfulness has been so pleasing in My sight as you have brought honor and glory to Me and to My Son Jesus.

You have stepped out in the boldness and courage that I have demanded of you and you have not wavered when you could so many times.

Miracles

Because of your faithfulness, and because of your dedication, and because of your obedience to obey Me at all cost, and even at the cost of the conveniences that many take for granted, I have set my angels loose to bring unto you those things that you have asked me for and I will see to it that every need you have is met.

I have placed with you spirits of tenderness and gentleness and supernatural love for My people.

In the Spiritual realm, you will see the manifestation of those things that I have shown you in your spirit. You will see the signs and wonders and miracles increase as you desire.

I will send you help in every area that you have need of and I will never fail you in any area. Because you have humbled yourself for My Namesake and because you have not feared men, but feared Me and stepped out in obedience at My command, I am increasing the anointing so that you will be able to rise above each and every situation that confronts you via the enemy, and you will overtake him and overrun him in every area.

Deena, I not only want you to travel with Gary but I intend to involve you more in areas of the ministry. You will sit back no longer.

I have placed an anointing upon you and I will involve you more and more in the ministry.

INTRODUCTION

For you have been faithful to stand by your husband as I used him. You have stood fast and helped even though many things were so hard. I have made you mighty in spirit and mighty in My power, saith God. You will arise and stand with your husband in a new and different way. Step out for I will not fail you and you will see more of the manifestation of My Spirit.

Your faithfulness and your obedience to Me have birthed a new strength and a faith that few have tasted. Step forward, saith God, for you will not be in the background any longer but you will move forward. There are those who hunger and thirst for what you have to give them. Many will seek you out for I am sending them to you to meet a need that only you can meet. I will give you a Word of Encouragement or whatever they need.

To Gary and Deena: You have humbled yourself before Me time and time again and you both have honored Me and uplifted My Son Jesus to so many and the time has come for you to receive your harvest.

— Prophecy Given to Gary and Deena at The Tabernacle in Crosby, Texas.

A Word to my wife Deena from a letter sent to us after a revival in Crosby, Texas.

Dear Deena:

I just wanted to let you know just how much of a blessing you are to the Body of Christ. You are a fine example of what a Godly woman should strive to be.

Just as the Father looked carefully to select the woman to bring forth His Son and accomplish His will on the earth, so also He selected a woman just as fitting to be a compliment unto Gary. Surely God uses him mightily and much of this is due to you his helpmate. I have seen you in the good times and the bad and surely you remain faithful.

(I Cor. 15:58) "Be ye steadfast unmovable; always abounding in the work of the Lord. For your work in the Lord has not been in vain."

Surely this scripture is written for you.

After giving my testimony on TV, Prophet Ron Smith sent this word to me:

Beloved Gary:

Your Channel 22 exposé was awesome. There was such an aura of God emanating from your very pores. Almost two hours seemed only like a moment. What you beheld in those unbelievable "snapshots" of glory was so striking that it would make sinners tremble and saints repent.

6

Gary, it explained to me why false witnesses would arise to discredit, defame, and destroy the credibility of your "in His presence" experience.

Like begets like. Thus you had parables that Daniel, John the Revelator, and the Apostle Paul describe in their times of rapturous ecstasy.

I encourage you to proclaim this from the housetops, mountaintops, and on the airwaves. I'm believing a book will be written and pamphlets printed. Russia, China, unborn nations need to hear it. Wow! It's hot! It's cool! It's medicine! It's light! It's incense!

It's manna! It's treasure!

– Ron Smith

Prophet of God

MIRACLES

The most important thing in your life is a miracle, especially when you need one. The Bible says Jesus Christ is the same yesterday, today and forever. The God we serve is a God of Miracles. If you take miracles out of the Word of God, then you have nothing but pulp bound by leather. Jesus spent over two-thirds of His life healing someone, coming from healing someone, or going to heal someone.

The scriptures testify it is God's desire to touch you and make you whole. Behold, I am the Lord, the God of all flesh: Is there anything too hard for me? [Jeremiah 32:27] Jesus said, With God all things are possible. [Matthew 19:26] Don't limit God to only what man can do for you. Man can fail, but God never fails to keep His promises and He will do exceedingly abundantly above all we ask or think. [Ephesians 3:20]

Throughout the Scriptures, beginning with the healing of Abimelech and his household [Genesis 21] and ending with the description of the Tree of Life in the New Heaven whose leaves are for the Healing of the Nations [Revelation 22:2], the Word makes it clear that Divine Healing has been provided for all people of all nations, in every generation.

The truth is that Christ wills all to be healed; otherwise Jesus would never have suffered that horrible scourging in Pilate's Judgment Hall, before His crucifixion: By whose stripes ye were healed. [Isaiah 53:5; 1 Peter 2:24.] I have had people tell me they do not believe in miracles. You will when you need one. If you go to a church that does not believe in healing, go find one where they do believe and will anoint you with oil and pray the prayer of faith so you will be healed. It is important that you learn how to believe God for your healing before you get into a crisis situation.

Some of you reading this book have accepted Jesus Christ as your Savior. I believe before you finish this book, if you have not already, you will decide to spend eternity with Jesus and you will also accept Jesus as your Healer.

I go to the best doctor. He is never out on call. He never has to go back for any refresher courses. He knows the cure for every disease. There is no new disease that comes up that He has to research to find out what to do with it. His name is Jesus Christ, the Son of God.

In Malachi 3:6, the Word of God says, I am the Lord, I change not. The strongest proof that it is God's will to heal you is the fact that God has not changed. Whatever God has done for anyone in the past, He will do for everyone today, who meets the same conditions, for God is no respecter of persons. If God worked miracles in the past only, then He would be the God that "was" and the God that "is." I am glad to testify boldly that He is the "Great I Am." Right now, God is still saying, I am the Lord that healeth thee.

Jesus Christ came into the world to do the will of the Father. If healing the sick was not God's will, Jesus greatly displeased His heavenly Father. In John 89:29 Jesus said, for I do always those things that please him. God was "well pleased" with the work of Jesus.

The last words of Jesus to all believers were: Go into all the world and preach the gospel to every creature... everyone that believes shall lay hands on the sick, and they shall recover. [Mark 16:15-18]

The most important thing in your life is a miracle, especially when you need one. The Bible says Jesus Christ is the same yesterday, today and forever. The God we serve is a God of Miracles. If you take miracles out of the Word of God, then you have nothing but pulp bound by leather. Jesus spent over two-thirds of His life healing someone, coming from healing someone, or going to heal someone.

The scriptures testify it is God's desire to touch you and make you whole. Behold, I am the Lord, the God of all flesh: Is there anything too hard for me? [Jeremiah

32:27] Jesus said, With God all things are possible. [Matthew 19:26] Don't limit God to only what man can do for you. Man can fail, but God never fails to keep His promises and He will do exceedingly abundantly above all we ask or think. [Ephesians 3:20]

Throughout the Scriptures, beginning with the healing of Abimelech and his household [Genesis 21] and ending with the description of the Tree of Life in the New Heaven whose leaves are for the Healing of the Nations [Revelation 22:2], the Word makes it clear that Divine Healing has been provided for all people of all nations, in every generation.

The truth is that Christ wills all to be healed; otherwise Jesus would never have suffered that horrible scourging in Pilate's Judgment Hall, before His crucifixion: By whose stripes ye were healed. [Isaiah 53:5; 1 Peter 2:24.] I have had people tell me they do not believe in miracles. You will when you need one. If you go to a church that does not believe in healing, go find one where they do believe and will anoint you with oil and pray the prayer of faith so you will be healed. It is important that you learn how to believe God for your healing before you get into a crisis situation.

Some of you reading this book have accepted Jesus Christ as your Savior. I believe before you finish this book, if you have not already, you will decide to spend eternity with Jesus and you will also accept Jesus as your Healer.

I go to the best doctor. He is never out on call. He never has to go back for any refresher courses. He knows the cure for every disease. There is no new disease that comes up that He has to research to find out what to do with it. His name is Jesus Christ, the Son of God.

In Malachi 3:6, the Word of God says, I am the Lord, I change not. The strongest proof that it is God's will to heal you is the fact that God has not changed. Whatever God has done for anyone in the past, He will do for everyone today, who meets the same conditions, for God is no respecter of persons. If God worked miracles in the past only, then He would be the God that "was" and the God that "is." I am glad to testify boldly that He is the "Great I Am." Right now, God is still saying, I am the Lord that healeth thee.

Jesus Christ came into the world to do the will of the Father. If healing the sick was not God's will, Jesus greatly displeased His heavenly Father. In John 89:29 Jesus said, for I do always those things that please him. God was "well pleased" with the work of Jesus.

The last words of Jesus to all believers were: Go into all the world and preach the gospel to every creature... everyone that believes shall lay hands on the sick, and they shall recover. [Mark 16:15-18]

There are many that do not believe in healing and miracles. If you believe it won't happen to you, then it won't. Your only other option is to go to the doctor. I am not anti-doctor. I respect doctors. They work hard to earn their degree and labor many hours to help people get well, but they are not God. If they say you are going to die of an incurable disease, you can believe that report, or you can believe the Word of God when it says, He shall take sickness away from the midst of thee. [Exodus 23:25] When Jesus is present nothing is impossible to them that believe and act accordingly. [John 14:14; Matthew 17:20]

Jesus promised to be with us to the end of the world. Lo, I am with you always, even unto the end of the world. [Matthew 28:20] Notice, this does not say that miracles would cease when the disciples died! We should expect miracles and healings unto the end of the age for the same compassionate Jesus who healed all that had need of healing, still wants to do the same thing today!

The same Spirit that anointed Jesus to preach deliverance to the captives, and recovery of sight to the blind, to set at liberty them that are bound [Luke 4:18] was poured out on every believer on the day of Pentecost and has never been withdrawn from the church.

Miracles give proof that Jesus is alive. If Jesus was not alive, His name would have no power to heal the sick and perform miracles. Before Jesus started healing people, no one troubled to follow Him anywhere. He had ministered in the synagogue before, but when He cast the demon out of the man in Luke 4:33-36, all the people were amazed at the authority and power His words possessed. The story of what He had done spread like wildfire into every part of the country around that region and many believed on Him when they saw His miracles. Jesus said in John 10:37-38: If I do not the works of my Father, believe me not. But if I do, though ye believe not me, believe the works: that ye may know, and believe that the Father is in me and I in him.

The Bible clearly shows that it is God's will to heal you. You can only receive from God to the extent of your belief. It's time for God's people to realize that when Jesus Christ died at Calvary, He died that you might be set free spiritually, physically, mentally, and financially.

If you look in a Greek dictionary, you will find that the word "sozo" [Romans 10:13] means saved, healed, and delivered. It is all available for you. It means that you were spiritually and physically made whole and delivered.

How can you preach Jesus unless you tell what He did and what He says? He still wants to do miracles for all who believe in Him. Wherever Jesus went, He was moved with compassion and healed all the sick that came unto Him. It is God's will for you to be healthy and whole. You may not receive a miracle instantly, but you will recover. He said that believers shall lay hands on the sick and they shall recover. Recovery is a progressive thing.

Many have been taught in their churches that God puts sickness on His children to teach them a lesson and is glorified as a result. How ridiculous! How long do you have to be sick and in pain before you learn your lesson? Once you learn it, it's time to be healed, right? I have never heard anyone stand up in church and say, "Thank You, God for giving me cancer or crippling my body with pain." NEVER! I don't know about you, but I have never been sick or in pain and it was good. Have you ever had your chest stopped up with infection, a sore throat, and throbbing headache, and believed it was good for you?

If it is God's will for you and I to be sick, then are we going against God's will if we go to a doctor? Thank God for doctors and nurses and the knowledge they have and the ability to help us. If it is God's will for you to be sick, then you should not go to the doctor or take medicine to get well. Aren't our traditions stupid?

On February 28, 1996, in Ft. Wayne, Indiana, I had a heart attack. Earlier that year, I had visited my natural father's grave and saw that he had died at the same age I was at that time. The devil jumped in the car with me, and whispered in my ear that I would die before I reached my next birthday. Fear will paralyze you. It will seize you by the throat with an iron grip, and you know you must have a miracle or you will die. I was in the hospital on the day before my birthday, and I stayed up until one minute past twelve, and got out of my bed, threw my arms up into the air and said, "Devil, I will live and not die and decree and declare the works of the Lord." The Word of God that you speak is alive and full of power. It is active and operative. It energized me and brought healing to my flesh. Hallelujah! The doctor told me the left lower ventricle of my heart was damaged beyond repair and I'd be on medication the rest of my life.

In 1998, the devil once again, brought the pain back. On August 31st, I had a heart catherization in Houston, Texas. The doctor ran the first part of the test and said, "When you die you need to leave your arteries to someone."

I told him, "I was not planning on dying."

He ran the second part of the test and said, "You have the best heart I've ever seen in my medical profession." He said he saw no scar tissue from the heart attack.

He ran the third part of the test and asked me what I did for a living.

I told him, "I'm an Evangelist."

He asked if I preached like Billy Graham and I told him I preached salvation like he did.

The doctor said, "Do you believe in healing?"

"Yes," I said.

"Do you have people praying for you?" he asked.

"Yes I do, all over the United States."

The doctor said, "Well son, you just got a miracle. Your arteries are crystal clear."

PRAISE GOD! I was healed and taken off medications I had been on for two years.

When you are under attack, you have to learn to fight with your spirit. I said, "Devil, you are a liar. Jesus has healed me. I am not going to put up with this anymore." The Bible says greater is He that is in us than he that is in the world. [1 John 4:4] There is a song that says that we went to the enemy's camp and took back what he stole from us. All of us that are born again have Christ living inside us and we can take back what the enemy has stolen from us.

Sickness was not part of God's original plan. There was no sickness or disease in the Garden of Eden. When Adam and Eve sinned, sickness and disease came upon them.

Thank God when Jesus Christ, the Son of God came forth from the grave, He bought us freedom from sickness and disease. The Bible says God made man in

His image. [Genesis 1:26] God is not sick with sugar diabetes, arthritis, cancer, or blood disease, and He did not put any of those things upon us. The devil's purpose is to steal, kill, and destroy. Jesus has redeemed us from the curse of the law. You do not have to be sick anymore. God has a miracle for you. Accept your miracle and be whole. Proverbs 3:1-2 says, My son, forget not my law for length of days, and long life shall it add to you.

GOD'S WORD IS MEDICINE

Many people say, "Well, in my opinion, I believe healing is not for today." You are then saying that your opinion is more important that what God thinks. It doesn't matter what your grandparents, parents, relative, and even the pastor of your church says. All that matters is what God ways. God has never been wrong. His word is pure truth.

Proverbs 4:22 says, The word of God is life to those that find them and health to all of their flesh. There is power in the Word of God. Just hearing it builds up your faith. "Behold, I will bring it health and cure, and I will cure them, and will reveal unto them the abundance of peace and truth." [Jeremiah 33:6]

Just begin to confess that the Lord is healing you right now. Jesus wants you well more than you want to be well. Don't let sickness talk you into letting it stay in your body.

In the Living Translation, Psalms 107:20-22 says, He spoke and they were healed, snatched from the door of death. Let them praise the Lord for His great love and for all his wonderful deeds to them. Let them offer sacrifices of thanksgiving and sing joyfully about His glorious acts.

Right now, just as Paul and Silas sang in the prison, start singing, "Bless the Lord O My Soul", "How Great Thou Art", "Great is the Lord" and "Greatly To Be Praised", and then just worship the Lord with the song. Allelujah.

Proverbs 3:1-2 says, My son forget not my law for length of days and long life shall it add to you. As you read and meditate on it, joy will come forth, and the joy of the Lord is your strength. [Nehemiah 8:10] Doctors have actually discovered that laughter releases healing hormones that drive out sickness and disease from your body.

I was preaching in Dallas, Texas and was asked to go to the hospital and pray for a lady who was dying of cancer. I found her room and opened the door. I was really taken by surprise because I was not expecting what I saw. A lady in her 40s was sitting on the edge of the bed holding a wig in her hand and laughing hysterically. She was completely bald; what a sight I saw. Laughter is contagious and soon I was laughing with her. As she lifted the wig into the air laughing, she said, "Devil, I will live and not die and decree and declare the works of the Lord." You could just feel the awesome presence of the Lord in that hospital room.

I introduced myself to her and told her that I had been asked to come pray for her. She taught me a powerful lesson that I have never forgotten. She said very kindly but firmly, "I don't know you or what you believe. I need a miracle and I don't just let anyone lay hands on me." You see, when you need a miracle, you must have someone agree with you. They must have the same faith you have or greater faith than yours to come into agreement with you. I told her my testimony—how I had died and went to heaven and was sent back to make Jesus real to people just like her in the condition she was in. She said, "You qualify." I laid hands on her and prayed the prayer of faith and then we just laughed together.

I heard someone crying and turned to see another lady in the room. I had not been aware that she was there. I asked her if I could pray with her. She told me that she was the lady's sister and that the doctor had just come into the room and told them that her sister only had a few days to live. She said, "Whoever it is that can make my sister laugh, when she received that kind of report, I want to know Him." I had the privilege to lead her to Jesus and she was born again. Then we were all rejoicing and laughing as the joy of the Lord filled that room. It was hard to leave, but I had to go to prepare to minister that night.

Several months later, I was back in Dallas ministering again and a lady with beautiful thick black hair came up to see me. She asked me if I remembered her. I told her I was sorry, although she looked familiar, I could not remember her. She started laughing and I said, "Oh yeah." She laughed at the devil and the joy of the Lord gave her strength to receive a miracle. Psalms 42:11 says, Who is the health of my countenance, and my God. Psalms 105:37 says, He brought them forth also with silver and gold and there was not one feeble person among their tribes.

Cecil B. DeMille's picture, The Ten Commandments, pictured a blind man being led by a child out of Egypt. That was wrong because out of the 4 to 5 million of them that came out of Egypt, the Bible says there was not one feeble one among their tribes. They did not have any doctors or nurses, but they walked out whole.

1 John 3:8 says, For this purpose the Son of God was manifested that he might destroy the works of the devil. One translation says, Jesus came to liquidate the devil's assets. The devil has made people deaf, dumb, blind, lame, insane, etc. Jesus cast out the devil and destroyed the devil's work, and healed all who had been afflicted by the devil. It is God's will to heal you—NEVER DOUBT IT. Just lift your hands and praise God you are healed.

Exodus 15:25 says, "I will take sickness away from the midst of thee." It has always been God's will for His children to be free of sickness and disease.

Proverbs 4:20-22 says, My son, attend to my words; incline thine ear unto my sayings. Let them not depart from thine eyes. Keep them in the midst of thine heart. For they are life unto those that find them, and health to all their flesh.

As God's Word gets into your spirit, it becomes a spiritual cure. A doctor, in the natural, has you take medicine on a regular basis. You must apply God's Word to your circumstance or situation in order to receive a supernatural healing. God's Word will heal your body once it is planted in your spirit. It will manifest itself in your physical being.

Now remember, you usually don't get sick overnight and you may not always be healed overnight. We all love instant miracles, but sometimes, it does not come overnight. You must take time to meditate upon the Word of God to develop your faith. If you need to see a doctor until your faith is built up to receive a miracle, don't be condemned. Don't try to go beyond your faith level. Remember though, if God can heal you by taking medicine, then He definitely can heal you by prayer.

There is no place in the Bible where Jesus ever turned anyone away that came to Him and said, "I want to be healed." The same healing power that flowed through Jesus to heal people is available for you today.

Chris Drain, wife of Pastor Dale Drain of Calvary Temple in Edmond, Oklahoma, received a miracle from God. In 1985, she was experiencing much difficulty breathing. Every breath she took was difficult. Here's her story.

My husband Dale and I learned that an Evangelist, by the name of Gary Wood, was ministering at another church in Edmond. We decided to attend the service. Brother Gary prayed for me and I experienced a miraculous healing in my body. One year later, during a battle with pneumonia, the doctors wanted an X-ray of my lungs. I discovered that one of the wires was left in my sternum from open heart surgery and it had punctured one of my lungs. At the time that Brother Gary prayed for me neither one of us knew what the problem was but God knew and used Gary as an instrument to heal my body! I praise the Lord for Brother Gary's ministry.

Psalms 103:1-3 in the NLV says, Praise the Lord I tell myself: with my whole heart I will praise His Holy Name. Praise the Lord, I tell myself, and never forget the good things He does for me. He forgives all my sins and heals all my diseases. This scripture shows that you are a physical and spiritual being, and God has provided for both of them. When the sin problems fall in line, then there is healing for the body.

Unconfessed sin will stop the miracle power of God in your life. Many people have unforgiveness in their heart, a critical spirit, rebellion against spiritual authority, bitterness, and resentment. Satan has access to your soul if you are involved in the occult, witchcraft, pornography, idolatry, drugs, and rock music. Many folks get up in the morning and the first thing they do is check the astrology column to see what they are to do that day. That's wrong and it opens you up for the devil to put sickness on your body and eventually destroy your soul. Here's an excellent example of the above principle:

I was ministering with Brother Charles Reed on KMCT-TV, Monroe, Louisiana. We were sharing the salvation prayer at the close of the Fully Alive Program. All the phone counselors had left the phones as the credits were running on the TV screen. The counselors were joining together to pray over the needs that had been called in during the program. The phone rang and our daughter Angel Wood answered the phone and the lady she prayed with accepted the Lord as her personal Savior and then received the baptism in the Holy Spirit with the evidence of speaking in tongues.

Now I have to interject here that our daughter was born mentally retarded. We were told she could not remember three things in a row and do a variety of things. God had marvelously healed her mind and body and she loves to share her testimony. Doctors wrote her off, but Jesus provided for her healing. She has her own business and has written a book called Angel, A Walking Miracle. Her ministry to this woman is a miracle in itself!

We were in the midst of a telethon at the station. The next day, Barbara Pritchard, the main counselor, told us what happened. She called the lady, who lives in Bastrop, LA, to verify the information such as: correct address, name, etc. To her amazement, the lady told her she had cut both her wrists and blood was dripping from her wrist at the time she had called the previous night. She felt an urge to turn on the TV. When she did, she saw us leading in the salvation prayer. She called the number on the screen. As she prayed with Angel for salvation, the blood stopped dripping completely from her wrist.

God is a merciful and miracle working God! Praise His Holy Name!

Billy Normington from Broadhead, Wisconsin, wrote to me after I had held a revival at Pastor Mark Pederson's church. These are the very words that every young person should pay attention to:

Thank you, Gary. Your message on rock music was a blessing to me. I spent a great part of my life listening to rock music not knowing the spiritual ramifications of it. I've been saved for 8 of my 37 years on this earth. I had kept a lot of this music in my home, not listening to it. But, it was still at my home. This stuff had become a part of my soul. Through your obedience to God, He released my soul from this music. I chose to make my home God's home and this garbage has no place in His or mine. Also, I would say to all young people, please don't be deceived by ungodly music. It does include drugs, perversion, and anger. God bless you, Gary for preaching the truth.

Cathy Davis of LaPorte, Texas wrote me this inspiring letter:

I wanted you to know how blessed I feel for having had my faith built and established under your ministry early in my Christian walk.

Eighteen and a half years ago, I was a fairly new believer, (I have been saved as a teenager, but I was new to the idea of a living, active God) learning wonderful things about the Lord under Brother Bryan Morrison at the Church of the Living Water in Deer Park, Texas. Brother Bryan's wife, Margaret (who's really an angel disguised as a human) invited my mother and me to accompany her to a "Women's Aglow" service with a marvelous minister named Gary Wood. At that time I was the 23 year old mother of two boys, Jason, a 2 years old, and Aaron, who was then about five months old. Aaron had been sickly since birth. From the beginning he has thrown up everything we gave him. He was severely anemic, underweight and pale. The only advice the doctors had given us was to feed him a half ounce of formula every half-hour. But even small amounts came right back up.

With that kind of schedule, both my baby and I were exhausted most of the time—just to try to keep him from starving! During the Aglow meeting, I felt my belief and faith grow enormously. As I listened to your testimony and ministry I thought to myself, "If God can do it for him, He can do it for me." When I took Aaron up front for prayer, you had a word of knowledge that he had a "blocked esophagus" and told me that God had healed it and I should take him home and feed him a good meal. I hadn't even told you about his problem! So of course, I believed that was straight from God and I took him home and fed him chili and crackers that very night. Aaron never had another problem with eating again. Today he is a 6-ft tall, 180 lbs., 19-year-old with a gentle spirit and lovely countenance as it should be with someone who has been touched by God.

My faith was built up firmly by that experience so when 2 years later my newest baby son, Timothy, developed spinal meningitis and slipped into a coma with 105° fever, I had no problem ignoring the doctors' "no hope" verdict and turning straight to God for his healing. When friends rushed to comfort me at the hospital they found me sitting by his bed calm and smiling. I wound up witnessing to them! The doctors were amazed when he came out of his coma and kept saying he shouldn't be alive. They then tried to warn me that his brain had probably been damaged and I should expect him to be blind, deaf, or retarded or all of it! I told them god had healed him, not them, and He didn't do things halfway. Today, Timmy is 16 years old, a healthy handsome junior in high school, making good grades, who witnesses and leads other students to the Lord. He plans on being a youth minister after college.

All three of my sons have been a blessing and a joy to their father and me. I can't imagine life without them and I thank God that I was there that night when you preached and prayed and started me down the road of sound faith in an alive, compassionate, real God!

In a typical ripple effect, many people that saw what God did for my sons, were able to believe when they had a crisis in their lives. In addition, my sons have seen many salvations with their teenage friends. Timmy even saved a baby from drowning. Imagine all the lives that would not be here and all the souls still in conflict if my

31

sons had died when they were babies instead of being healed by God through faith and belief that started with your ministry and prayers. Once again, I thank you, Gary and I thank God for you. Ours is only one story in probably many hundreds of lives that you have influenced and touched. Imagine the ripple effect on that many people. Thanks for being obedient when God called you to your ministry. You will probably never know just how far you've reached… and it's going on!

The same Jesus who walked upon this earth is ready to save you and heal you right now. Healing belongs to you now. It is a gift. Forgiveness of sins comes first then healing for our disease follows it. God gave Jesus to take your judgment and what you deserve.

One time in a counseling session, a young man said to me, "Preacher, just give me what I deserve."

"You deserve death, judgment, and hell," I said. "Thank God He commendeth His love toward us in that while we were yet sinners,

He died for us."

I led him to Jesus. Jesus Christ became sin on our behalf so that we might share the life of God. [2 Corinthians 5:21] Receive abundant life right now.

THE GREATEST MIRACLE

Miracles gave BOLDNESS to the believers and disciples to preach Christ to the unbelievers. [Acts 4:29-30] The miracle convinced and convicted men of their sins. In Acts 4:4; 5:14, five thousand people were convicted in one day because of one miracle! Miracles helped spread the gospel faster! [Acts 5:14-16]

Everywhere the disciples preached, God would confirm His word with miracles, signs, and wonders, causing multitudes to turn to Christ.

In Acts 8:5-8, the city of Samaria gave heed unto those things which Philip spoke, hearing and seeing the miracles which he did.

For unclean sprits, crying with loud voice, came out of may that were possessed with them: and were taken with palsies, and that were lame, were healed. And there was great joy in that city.

All the inhabitants of Sharon and Lydda turned to the Lord when Peter told Aeneas, which had kept his bed eight years, sick of the palsy, Jesus Christ maketh thee whole. Arise and make thy bed.

And he arose immediately. [Acts 9:32-35]

Many believed in Joppa when Peter raised Dorcas from the dead. [Acts 9:42]

And by the hands of the apostles were many signs and wonders wrought among the people... and believers were the more added to the Lord, multitudes both of men and women. Insomuch that they brought froth the sick into the streets, and laid them on beds and couches, that at the least the shadow of Peter passing by might overshadow some of them. There came also a multitude out of the cities round about unto Jerusalem bringing sick folks, and them which were vexed with unclean spirits; and they were healed everyone. [Acts 5:12-16]

The book of Acts closes with miracles in full swing even to a heathen king... the father of Publius lay sick of a fever and of a bloody flux: to whom Paul entered in, and prayed, and laid his hands on him, and healed him. So when this was done, others also, which had diseases on the island, came and were healed. [Acts28:8-9]

When the heathen saw Publius' father healed, they concluded that if God would heal one, He was able and willing to heal everyone who had need of healing!

The greatest miracle that can happen to anyone is recorded in John 3: There was a man of the Pharisees, named Nicodemus, a ruler of the Jews. The same came to Jesus by night, and said unto him "Rabbi, we know that thou are a teacher come from God; for no man can do these miracles that thou doest, except God be with him."

Jesus answered and said unto him, "Verily, verily I say unto thee, except a man be born again, he cannot see the kingdom of God." Nicodemus saith unto him, "How can a man be born when he is old? Can he enter the second time in his mother's womb and be born?"

Jesus answered, "Verily, verily I say unto thee, except a man be born of water and of the Spirit, he cannot enter into the kingdom of

God. That which is born of the flesh is flesh; and that which is born of the Spirit is spirit. Marvel not that I said unto thee, Ye must be born again." [John 3:1-7]

Jesus is having a conversation with a man named Nicodemus. Jesus said, in essence, Nicodemus, you are all wrong, and you need to get right. Had Jesus spoken these words to anyone else, it would not have seemed so strange as when he spoke them to a man of such character as Nicodemus. If a man like Nicodemus needed to be born again, how much more do each of us need this experience?

Nicodemus was a Pharisee. He believed in the resurrection. He was over fifty years old, mature and an established man in the community. He came to see Jesus by night and recognizing that Jesus performed mighty miracles, he wanted to know how he could be born again. Nicodemus was confused and thought that he would have to go back into his mother's womb and be born of the flesh, but Jesus said that it was a spiritual birth, not a physical birth that he needed. To be born again means that your spirit is recreated into the image of Jesus.

Had Jesus spoken these words to the woman at the well who had five husbands, it would not nearly have seemed as strange as when spoken to Nicodemus. If he had told the woman caught in the act of adultery "you must be born again," surely, we would all agree. But Nicodemus was really like the mayor of the city. He belonged to the country club of his day and was a good man.

Let us notice some things about Nicodemus:

1) Nicodemus was an educated man. He was a master of Israel. He had a degree. Education without God is in vain. I thank God for my education. I was a very promising student. I promised my parents every report care I would do better. I was an outstanding student as well. I was usually 'out-standing' in the hall watching the girls go by. If you take a thief that will steal the hubcaps off your car, and educate that dude, without a change of heart, he will then steal your whole car. Education is not the answer to man's problems. If education would have solved life's problems, we would have solved them a long time ago.

2) Nicodemus was a good moral man. He was a Pharisee and prayed three times a day. Your name may be on the church roll, and you may tithe all of your income for the year, but if you are not on God's roll, your ultimate destination is hell. It takes Jesus to keep you out of hell. Each individual must receive Christ. You cannot go on Mom's faith, or the fact that your dad is a deacon. It must be a personal commitment of your own.

I saw an ad in the newspaper that read TICKETS TO HEAVEN. It said no matter how good or bad you have been in the past, or will be in the future, this ticket is guaranteed by God to get you into heaven. The person writing the ad said that he'd had a dream that God came to sell them for $1.00 each. He said that God would like to know if there are 100,000 people that believe in Him enough to accept His offer. This could be God's greatest gift to you. To order your ticket, send $1.00 (cash only) and a self-addressed stamped envelope and then gave the address. The person who wrote this is so miserably deceived. Only Jesus can guarantee that you will go to heaven.

3) Nicodemus could not physically be born into the Kingdom of heaven. Being born in America does not make you a Christian. A Jew born under the covenant of relationship of God has to be saved. Nicodemus had to be born again. You cannot get good enough to go to

heaven. The Bible says there is none righteous, not even one, for all have sinned and fallen short of the glory of God. [Romans 3:11,23]

You do not need reformation, but transformation. Reformation is like white washing a rotten fence. The problem is on the inside. Jesus wants to save you as you are. It takes more than a change in exterior circumstances to make a difference in a person's life. After you come and get born again, Jesus will help you quit doing those things that are a problem in you life. You don't quit doing evil things and then come to Jesus, but you come to Jesus and He will help you to quit doing evil things.

Joining a church and being baptized in water cannot save you. No church or organization can save you. Water will not wash away dirt without a little soap. So how is it going to wash away your sin?

The old song "What Can Wash Away My Sin?" Nothing but the blood of Jesus is the answer! Baptism is being obedient to God's Word. You get baptized because you have been saved, not to get saved. You can be baptized unto you know every fish by its first name, but it will not wash away you sin. It takes the blood of Jesus.

WHAT DOES IT MEAN TO BE BORN AGAIN?

There is a divine change that occurs in a man's nature. God makes this change in you. Jesus saves you. I cannot save anyone and neither can you. Titus 3:5 says, He saved us, not on the basis of deeds which we have done in righteousness, but according to his mercy, by the washing of regeneration and renewing of the Holy Spirit whom he poured out upon us richly through Jesus Christ our Savior. It is a complete change. Therefore if any man be in Christ, he is a new creature, behold old things are passed away, all things become new. [2 Corinthians 5:17] The blood of Jesus cleanses us from all sin. This is an instantaneous act of God. Whosoever shall call upon the name of the Lord shall be saved. [Romans 10:13]

WHY DO WE NEED SALVATION?

All of us are like sheep gone astray. Each of us has turned to his own way. [Isaiah 53:6] All have sinned and come short of the glory of God. [Romans 3:23] There is none righteous, no not one. [Romans 3:10] That is why we have to have police. If everyone were born again and served the Lord, there would be no need for the police. You could leave your keys in the car without fear of someone stealing it. We have banks to put our money in because, if we walked around with large sums of money in our pockets, a thief would steal it from you. I have two children. I never had to teach them to do wrong as children or adults. It was their nature to be disobedient. The Bible says we are by nature the children of wrath. [Ephesians 2:3] We have depraved nature. Our nature must be changed. You can take a pig out of a pigpen, clean him up, put a bow in his hair and even paint his fingernails, but he is still a pig; and as soon as he can, he will go back to wallowing in the mud.

You need to be born again because of what Jesus did on the cross. The cross requires us to be born again. Jesus gave His life that we might be born again. Jesus said, I am the way, the truth, and the life. [John 14:6] Without Him there is no going and no knowing. Without Him there is no living. We cannot be born again by our good works.

The Bible says in Romans 5:8: God commendeth his love toward us in that while we were still sinners, Christ died for us. God is a God of love. God is Holy. God's Nature demands payment for sin. Jesus took the death and hell you and I deserve and conquered it for us. Jesus said, "I am the door, if any man would like to enter any other way, he is a thief and a robber." There is one God; one Jesus, the mediator and substitute for our sins.

WHAT ARE THE BENEFITS OF BEING BORN AGAIN?

Jesus will forgive the past. In Christ, you have become a new creature. Old things are passed away; and all things have become new. In Christ you stand righteous in the sight of God—as though you had never sinned in your life. God looks at you through the blood of Jesus, and accepts the blood of Jesus as payment for your sins. Not only does Christ forgive your past sins, but also, He helps you in the present by being your advocate to the Father. [1 John 2:1] Receiving Christ is the only way to live victoriously. Philippians 4:13 says, I can do all things through Christ which strengthens me.

WHEN SHOULD ONE BE BORN AGAIN?

The Bible says, Behold now is the accepted time; behold now is the day of salvation. [2 Corinthians 6:2] If I were to ask you if you planned on going to hell, you would look at me and tell me that you have no intention of going to hell. The road to hell is paved with good intentions. Everyone that goes to hell doesn't plan on being there. I urge you to receive Jesus Christ as Savior. The resource of the Christian life, my friend, is Jesus Christ. Jesus said, He that believeth on me, as the scripture hath said, out of his belly shall flow rivers of living water. [John 7:38] The apostle Paul wrote, for me to live is Christ... [Philippians 1:21] Right now you can receive Christ. I urge you to pray this prayer and ask Him to come into your heart:

Dear Lord Jesus:

If never before, right now I ask you through your precious blood that was shed on Calvary's cross to cleanse me from all my sins. I receive you as my Savior and Lord. God, be merciful to me, a sinner, and save my soul. Thank You, Jesus, for coming into my heart, and now I will serve you and live for you.

SOMETHING TO THINK ABOUT..."WITH THE HELP OF GOD, CHIP IT AWAY!"

Have you heard the story about the man who had a huge boulder in his front yard? He grew weary of this big unattractive stone being the centerpiece of his lawn, so he decided to make a victory of it, and turn the big stone into a work of art. He went to work on it with a hammer and chisel. He chipped away at the big boulder until it became a beautiful stone elephant. When he finished, it was gorgeous, breath-taking… and a neighbor asked, "How did you ever carve such a marvelous likeness of an elephant?"

The man answered, "I just chipped away everything that didn't look like an elephant!"

If you have anything in your life right now that does not look like Jesus then, with the help of God, chip it away! If you have hatred, prejudice, vengeance, or envy in your heart, get rid of it right now! Let God chip everything out of your life that does not look like Jesus.

Pastor Freddy Hall of Dineah Christian Center in Shiprock, New Mexico, recently called me to tell me this exciting story.

Pastor Hall and his wife work with the Navajo Indians, and have a church that has grown from four people to over four hundred in 25 months!

A contractor named Sheldon Burke came to him after reading a book on hell. It scared him and he asked Pastor Hall if what he read was true. The pastor assured him it was, and probably, a whole lot worse than what he had read in the book. Sheldon asked if the pastor had anything else he could read and Fred gave him my book A Place Called Heaven. After he read it, he came back the next day and was ready to receive Jesus Christ as his Savior.

THIS IS THE GREATEST MIRACLE! Sheldon was instrumental in bringing his brother and his family to Christ.

Terry Weber wrote me this thrilling testimony of her son's deliverance:

When you were at Trinity Church in Houston, TX, my 21 year old son went forward and recommitted his life to Jesus, and the Lord completely changed him. Hallelujah! He was delivered from drugs, alcohol, and cigarettes. He says he doesn't have any desire for his previous daily habits, which he had about six years. He has completely changed. There is a shine on his face now. He studies the Bible one on one with a young man at church, and goes to church every time the doors are open, and stays until they are closed. He joins the church activities. He has only Christian friends, and God keeps giving him more. He had been in a drug rehabilitation hospital for eight months, but was unable to quit drugs on his own. Jesus Christ completely healed him. Praise God!

I have my sweet natural son back. Today is my birthday and this is the greatest gift possible. It's so neat to watch him grow in the Lord. Jesus changed our son. No one was able to change him. Jesus did a complete work on him. Praise the Lord.

Betty Weathersby wrote me this letter about her son's deliverance:

My son Kris had an evil spirit. He was rebellious, failing in school, fighting me, lying, stealing, cursing me, disobedient to all authority, and did many other ungodly things. Kris is nine years old and in the third grade. I told God either His Word was true or it's not, and now was the time for his deliverance. I know God was a deliverer. God used Gary Wood and the anointing upon his life to break the yoke of bondage over our son. He's free! He is a different child now. Praise God! THIS IS THE GREATEST MIRACLE!

Here is a letter dated January 17, 1999, from Vanessa Charlie:

Dear Gary Wood,

Thank you for sending us copies of your book. Out preacher is Brother Hall from Shiprock. I live in Kirkland. On this Sunday morning my mother Victoria Tsoise came back with your book and asked if I wanted to read it. I said OK and I did. I enjoyed it very much and accepted Jesus into my heart and prayed for the Holy Ghost. On Thursday (four days ago) my mother had a prayer meeting here and I watched while everybody prayed in tongues. I was amazed. So I prayed also that I would be like that, when I grow up or I mean now. I wanted what they had; peace, love, joy, understanding, and strength in the Lord and also in the Holy Spirit.

I prayed for four days and today I got your book (like fate). I guess your book changed my life and I'm excited to be a Christian and a full believer in God. I am sure your copies saved many people like me. I do believe the end is coming and I want to tell others about Christ. A long time ago I went to a woman's prayer meeting and a lady gave us little hearts that the kids in Sunday School had written for us. When I received mine I had my name on it which was the same as the little girl who wrote on it. It encouraged me to trust in God and trust that He will give me the strength to save many souls.

I understand it now and am excited to tell others. I also forgot to tell you my name. It is Vanessa Charlie. I believed in your book and God also. Thank you for sending it when I needed something to believe in. I also thank God because He was behind this.

Sincerely,

Vanessa

DIVINE HEALING FOR ALL

Ye shall know the truth and the truth shall make you free. [John 8:32] Since He created us, God knows more about our physical bodies than any earthly person does. Through the sacrifice of Jesus Christ, He has provided healing for all who are willing to receive it and meet the conditions. God can do more for us than any person. The Bible says, Behold, I am the Lord, the God of all flesh… IS THERE ANYTHING TOO HARD FOR ME? [Jeremiah 32:17]

In 1974, I was pastoring a Baptist church in New Mexico. Our little son David was playing around after church. He climbed on the car. He fell off the car and hit his head, and a large lump burst out on his head. Now, I knew medically that if a lump goes inward, it's much more serious than if it goes outward. I heard the Lord speak to me. I was to take David to the hospital. In the natural, his injury did not seem serious enough to take him to the hospital.

However, it was very strong in my spirit that I was to take him to receive medical assistance. We arrived at the hospital. We went through the emergency room entrance and were met by a man who was dressed like a doctor. He escorted us into an examining room. With his equipment he looked into David's eyes, ears, and nose. "It isn't there; that's not what I'm looking for," the man said. David was very calm through this whole process and there was peace in the room. He looked one more time up David's nose and said, "Yes, there it is; that's what I am looking for." David had been playing with a Bic pen and the tip of it came of when he shoved it up into his nose. The membranes were already growing around it. If the doctor had not discovered it, surgery would have been necessary. The doctor removed the obstacle without any problem or pain to David. David never cried.

We left and took David home very thankful that the doctor had found this object and removed it. The next day, I was visiting patients in the hospital and I went to the E.R. to thank the doctor who had treated our son. I found out he wasn't on duty. In fact, no one knew who he was. I have his name and description and was told no one by that name worked in the hospital. They showed me the records that said our family doctor had treated David the night before. Our family doctor was in a city over 200 miles away. You can believe whatever you want, but we believe God sent an angel to minister to our son. We never received a doctor bill. Now, THAT'S A MIRACLE!

I was 7 years old when I got my knee crushed in a car wreck and I've had a problem with it for 12 years, but Jesus healed me when Brother Gary prayed for me. Sherry Bishop — Jackson, Missouri

I came to Jackson, Missouri at Good News Christian Center, with Pastor Johnny Seabough. Kris J. King writes when she was around 11 years old: She had been having trouble with her eyes since she was 8 years old. She had just gotten new glasses and was having trouble with them fitting right. She got fed up with it and when I called people who wanted their eyesight prayed for to come forward, she came to the altar to receive prayer. After I prayed for her, she fell under the power of the Holy Spirit.

When she got up, she could see her mom and she said, "I can see; I can see!" Ever since that night she has not had to wear glasses. Ginger Brandon tells how I prayed with her at the altar and God told me He was healing her lungs. She chose to believe and receive her healing. Earlier, she had an X-ray that showed she had liquid and scar tissue on her lungs.

Her doctor called her and reminded her to get another chest X-ray to see what was happening. She had it done and the doctor sent her a letter saying her lungs were clear and there was no reason for concern. She wrote, "Thank you for your faith and faithfulness."

Miracles

In Ohio during a revival at Pastor O'Haire's church:

A brother and sister were healed. Ever since birth, Virginia L.Tebelman had been so plagued by food allergies that finding something she could eat was a challenge. She was prayed for on Monday night of the revival, and by Tuesday morning the blisters on her body, caused by an allergic reaction, were completely dried up. During the day, she ate chocolate, cherries, food with citrus, eggs, and several things that would have previously cause a severe reaction. She has not broken out, been sick, or had any reaction at all.

Ryan D. Tebelman fell face first on the sidewalk the Saturday before the meeting started. By Monday, a large wound on his forehead had become badly infected, and the area around his eye was swelling. He was prayed for that night for healing. On Tuesday morning when his mother went to change his bandage, there was no wound, not even a scab, only raw pink skin.

In Broadhead, Wisconsin:

Gary Caudell was healed of a sprained back and injured arm. God told me to put my foot on people's backs and necks, and they would be healed. I have discovered obedience creates an atmosphere to receive a miracle. If we obey God no matter how ridiculous it might seem, God will move to perform miracles. Jon

Kamlager had hurt her leg two years before I came to the church she attended, and she came up for prayer. She said the doctor couldn't do anything for her. She stood at the altar in faith watching people all around her getting healed. The power of Jesus was very strong in that service. The Lord spoke to me to have her bend her ankle seven times. Then, she went down under the power of the Spirit. When she got up, she was able to put all her weight on her bad leg, and there was no pain. Within minutes, she was doing things she had not been able to do for the past two years.

Jane Mconners is the pianist at Doyle Community Church in Foster, Oklahoma where her husband serves as a deacon. Pastor Jean Patterson has a precious group of people that our family looks forward to ministering to every time we are in Oklahoma: Jane wrote me and said she that for the past 12 years, she had been in chronic pain starting in her back and moving outward down her legs and arms. She had been that way since January 2, 1986, and sometimes she couldn't move. "I want to tell the world that on the 21st of July 1998, I was healed of chronic pain. I praise the Lord for my healing."

Pastor Perkins told the doctor that she had lots of people praying for her: The doctor said, "We know prayer helps. It was proven in a clinical study where the doctors literally put the names of all their patients in a jar. Half the patients were prayed for, but the other half were not. None of the patients were told about the study or the prayers. After the study was over, the physicians analyzed the results and the statistics proved that those patients prayed for recovered better and much faster than those not prayed for. That study was published in Texas Medical Association Journal. I want you to keep praying first and foremost!" Pastor Perkins was healed of a serious eye problem. We were in Houston, Texas, in a 38-week revival with Pastor Rodger and Georgeann Dewitt of New Covenant Praise Church.

Signs and wonders happen every week. Here are some of the amazing stories that happened during that time: Spastic colons were healed; blind eyes were opened; deaf ears unstopped; and people that were bound in wheelchairs got up and walked. People came from all over the city. One lady came at 2:30 for a 7:00 service to be sure to get a seat. She was healed of ulcers in her stomach and received the baptism of the Holy Spirit.

Helga shared how I prayed over her 17-year old daughter. She had 15 handicaps due to Agent Orange. One of them was that she was totally blind. She could hardly speak. God healed her and opened her eyes, and she began to talk clearly. She told the doctor that Jesus loved her. God healed her mind and she got a college education. Walter Bartect, a pharmacist in Humble, Texas, was in the service. I gave a Word of Knowledge for someone with impaired hearing. Walter knew that message was for him and he responded.

He came boldly to the front and said, "I want my ears to open tonight and I know Jesus loves me because I am His child and I want to receive a healing. Brother Gary did something foolish in the natural. He stuck his fingers in my ears and I could not hear at all. He began to pray and it seemed like minutes, but it was probably only a matter of seconds. The instant that he took his fingers out of my ears, I began to hear again in the ear which I had not heard any sound in for two years. I give Jesus all the praise and glory for that. The sound of music was so loud to my ears because I had not heard in two years, that I had to get away from the sound. I made every healing service for twelve weeks."

Pastor Dewitt relates:

When these healing meetings started, I was in the midst of a tremendous conflict. The devil tried to destroy me. The enemy wanted to abort the ministry. God gave us a message on Praise.

The enemy brought such an attack, that one Sunday night, I called Brother Gary and told him I wasn't coming to church that night. I even offered Brother Gary the church to pastor. I lay in bed, pulled the covers up to my neck, and I thought I'll just stay home. Then I realized we were having a miracle service, and said to myself, 'I've got to get up and get to the miracle service. 'From that day forward, God turned everything around because the oppression lifted and the devil's attack was stopped. From that day forth, God has led us from Glory to Glory.

We sang a song that said we are able to go up and take the country, to possess the land from Jordan to the sea: James had a stiff swollen knee and could hardly walk. The Lord told him if he got to the service that night he would get his healing.

We asked everyone to march around, and James obeyed. He said, "The Lord touched and healed me. All the pain as gone and the swelling went down immediately." God has chosen the foolish things to confound the wise. If you want a miracle, you need childlike faith. We make everything too difficult: One little girl named Teresa Prentis was in these anointed services, and sores all over her body instantly disappeared.

Jerry Switzer was in a wheelchair for fourteen weeks. It took a lot of effort for him to come to church. He had no transportation to come to church one Sunday, so he wheeled himself to church from where he lived about a mile away. Brother, that is determination to get a miracle. Can you imagine that? Some folks can't drive in an air-conditioned car and go to an air-conditioned church with comfortable chairs to sit on. Whatever it is you need, God is well able to supply it and meet your need. Jerry came and on the 15th week, he stood while I was preaching, and received his miracle. Praise God!

Grandview Assembly Church is located in Grandview, Missouri. The pastor is Bob Johnson. He has a deep love for the nation of Israel. This wonderful man of God and his wife Sonya take tours to the land of our Lord at least once a year. The church sent me there in 1985, and it changed my ministry. Every minister needs to go at least once in his or her lifetime. I was privileged to minister a "Week of Glory" in this great church, and here are some of the testimonies from that week: John and Connie Campbell were born again.

Red Martin, an automobile salesman, was filled with the Holy Ghost. Doris Robertson overcame an emotional fear. Judy Peters was healed of cancer after I prayed for her. Henry Peters was filled with the Holy Spirit.

One lady was going to commit suicide and God delivered her and filled her with His Spirit. One lady was healed in her kidney and her husband was born again. Annette's right eardrum was torn. Now, she can hear 100%. Kathy Brown was struggling with bitterness and God delivered her. Jim Brown had a pulled muscle and God healed him so he was able to play football that

Friday night. Susie received a healing in her back and found direction in her life.

Gale was healed in her emotions and she was set free from bondage. Whom the Son sets free is free indeed. Hallelujah! Doris was totally healed of dermatitis that she had for two weeks.

Rhonda brought her brother limping into the church and he was healed of a pinched nerve. She also brought 10 children to the Lord that week. Carolyn was praying and fasting for a friend's husband who had been an alcoholic for 11 years. He received salvation that week.

Sandy received a healing in her back. Stephanie was released from depression and set free. Jill was set free also from depression and God healed her back. Ava was set free from smoking cigarettes for 15 years and had a new hunger for His Word. Deena held onto over 40 rock music tapes. She did not want to give them up. After hearing a message I preached on rock music, she threw all the tapes away and was set free.

Chad had severe back pain and thought he would have to give up his job, but God healed him. John was baptized in the Holy Spirit. His wife teaches at the church school. Betty responded to a Word of Knowledge that someone was being healed of a condition where she could not smell. She had this condition for twelve years and God set her free. She could smell roses and things cooking on the stove.

Nancy Taylor was completely freed from the bondage of bitterness. Alan was born again. Nancy was afraid that if I touched her, she would fall in the Spirit, so she resisted coming down all week. Finally, on Friday night, she came to the altar and the Holy Spirit touched her and she was delivered from bondage in her past. Her soul was restored. The Lord ministered to her all night long.

Angie's six-year old son was delivered from an evil oppression that week. Jean had three cysts and they shrank. She had a neck injury and God healed her. She felt organs in her body moving and God restored her. She got a complete overhaul.

One man had polyps disappear on his colon after prayer. Another lady's feet were healed. Sister McNally was healed of scoliosis in her back that week. She had severe back pain and her back was aching but God healed her. Pastor Johnson explained in a message following this revival why God healed so many backs. He told how God had instructed me to put my foot on people's backs, and God did something like a chiropractic adjustment. He told me how I sought the Lord daily and came to the service going in the direction God told me to go.

Here are his words:

You don't find anywhere in the Bible where, when it's time to pray for backs, that you have people lay down and put your foot on them. That sounds dumb, stupid, and far out. It sounds just like what was recorded in 2 Kings 5. When Naaman went down to stand before the prophet Elisha, he thought Elisha would come out and put a cross of oil on his forehead, wave his hand, and in a very dignified way, pray over him. The Lord however told Elisha to tell Naaman to go to the river Jordan and jump in and out seven times.

Don't you know that sounds dumb, stupid, irrational, and makes no sense whatsoever. The secret was obeying God. Jesus did foolish things. He made mud out of spittle and put it on a blind man's eyes and told him to go to the pool of Salom. The secret of the man's healing was obedience. I agree totally with Pastor Johnson.

Kathy Cox was in pain in her back and God healed her to where she could wear heels again without hurting. May Lee had not been able to eat for about a month and a half. Her stomach was healed and she had her first hamburger that night. Michael Warner's son fell in the parking lot Sunday afternoon and hurt his leg very bad. Mike Grimes stopped his car and laid hands on the boy and he was instantly healed.

God wants to use ordinary people to bring His healing to others. He wants our availability, not just our ability. Randy Nash had swelling in his gums and he was healed. The most important thing that happened was that he received a compassionate heart to pray for his wife.

Janice had a bad temper and she gave it to the Lord. Her soul was restored. Her husband was freed from bitterness over a past divorce. Craig had been praying for transportation and God provided it for him. Someone took him aside one night and gave him two gold coins, which provided a financial need being met. He is still Jehova Jirah, our provider. You can have your miracle right now. Just believe and receive.

For those of you who have been oppressed, your oppression is coming to an end. For those that have been overcome by infirmity, your infirmities are coming to an end. For those that have been poverty stricken, your poverty is coming to an end. The heavens are going to open and the glory of God is going to fall upon His people. There is total freedom available for you today. If you are sad, happiness is available to you. If you're depressed, you can be blessed. Those in fear and doubt can come out. Those in poverty will have abundance. Those in mental oppression will receive peace of mind. Hallelujah! Hallelujah! Hallelujah!

GOD CAN AND HE WILL

GOD CAN AND HE WILL

When I was pastor of Full Gospel Fellowship of the Southwest in Stafford, Texas, we had many miracles occur. One case was a lady who had a lump on her breast. It was diagnosed as malignant. The doctors had scheduled a radical mastectomy for Cher. She came and had hands laid on her and received the prayer of faith. When she went back to the doctor, he told her that somehow a mistake had been made. Now there was no need for surgery because the lump was benign.

I remember a 59-year old man who came to our church from Baton Rouge, Louisiana. He was scheduled for surgery at the Veteran's Administration Hospital. The man had already had part of his tongue cut out because of throat cancer. The doctors had found more in his neck and throat. After prayer, he went to the hospital and they found all the cancer was gone.

One day, Ricky and Sophia Garcia walked into my office very frightened. They were requesting prayer for their young son, who was in the hospital in Galveston, diagnosed with leukemia. They talked to the priest at the church. He told them that I believed in praying for the sick. The came to Full Gospel and told me their story.

I was deeply touched and before I prayed for their son's healing, I had the privilege of leading them to the Lord. We then prayed for the healing of their son. As we were praying, I heard the Lord speak to me so softly and sweetly, saying that the boy was healed. I told them what I had heard from the Lord and they were excited. They arrived at John Sealy Hospital in Galveston, and went to their son. The doctors were trying to get in touch with them. At first, this frightened them. The doctors quickly calmed them and told them that there was a change in their son's condition. They requested permission to run further tests. Upon completion of those tests, they announced to the parents that there was no trace of leukemia in their son. Hallelujah!

God can turn any situation around. No matter how you feel, or how things look in the natural, if you will keep believing God and acting on His Word, He is ready and willing to give you a victory greater than you can ever imagine.

HEALTH BRINGS GLORY TO GOD

What? Know ye not that your body is the temple of the Holy Ghost which is in you, which ye have of God and ye are not your own? For ye are bought with a price: THEREFORE GLORIFY GOD IN YOUR BODY, AND IN

YOUR SPIRIT, WHICH ARE GOD'S. [1 Corinthians 6:19-20]

Our bodies belong to the Lord Jesus Christ for He has bought them. God doesn't get any glory out of your body being sick. If He did, WHY WOULD HE WANT YOU TO BE WELL?

Nancy Winkler from Bay City, Texas wrote:

I had suffered with headaches for years. They were getting so bad I remember many times laying and crying in desperation, "Lord, heal me or let me die." I decided to go to a chiropractor and there I learned from X-rays I had no spaces between the bones in my neck. The only relief I could get was constant chiropractic visits and periodic traction.

One night in a church service, the Lord revealed to Brother Wood that someone was suffering with neck and back problems and they had spent hundreds of dollars with a chiropractor. I went for prayer and was HEALED! Praise God, I felt great!

The very next day I had a car accident. After the shock and initial pain passed, I realized my neck was beginning to hurt. I kept asking, "Why God, you just healed me. Why did that woman have to hit me?" Everyone insisted I go to the chiropractor for X-rays. They could not be taken until the following day because of swelling, so I waited. When I returned for my X-rays, the doctor assured me that I would have great damage to my neck since the car was totaled out. "You'll have to come every day for visits and therapy," said the doctor, preparing me for the worst.

My best friend was the X-ray technician so I got to stay in the dark room with her while they developed the X-rays. As she pulled each X-ray out she would say, "Perfect!" We returned to the room with the doctor and he again began to talk about how bad it must be. He turned to look over the X-rays so he could point out just how serious it was. Instead he was almost speechless. All he could say was, "Well there's not much I can say; your neck looks perfect!" I have spaces between my vertebrae. I have never had. Hallelujah! God spared me from any harm in a rather major accident and showed us all I have a brand new neck!

C.B. Johnson of San Angelo wrote these words after God healed him:

I am a computer technician who has worked on and programmed computers for over 15 years. I consulted with a neurologist who suspected that I had damaged a main nerve in my right wrist. The condition is commonly known as CARPAL TUNNEL SYNDROME. It results in damage to the carpal nerve, which is the main nerve in the hand. It is very painful and numbness follows. After a week of heavy medication and wearing a wrist brace I came to a meeting Gary Wood was conducting. The Lord strengthened my wrist and I took off my brace. I give glory to the Lord for healing me.

"Cotton" from Cape Girardeau, Missouri shared his testimony with me:

I was a railroader for 42 years and all the loud noise of the trains damaged my hearing, so badly, that I finally had to wear hearing aids in both ears. I went up for prayer on Monday night of the meeting and it seemed nothing happened. I went home and went to bed and about two o'clock in the morning I got up to let our little dog outside. All at once, I heard all the sounds around me; clock ticking, refrigerator running, dog barking off in the distance and many more sounds. I hadn't been able to hear for the past year. I could hear without a hearing aid. Praise God!

I have a prescription from Dr. Garcia from Corpus Christi, Texas that certifies Janie Cooper is no longer a diabetic after she received prayer for healing. Thank You, Jesus.

Miracles

Francene Sulak from East Bernard, Texas wrote after a meeting at Friendship Assembly in East Bernard:

Brother Wood was told by God that someone in the audience needed their teeth cleaned. Just days before my husband and I had been considering having our teeth cleaned. I told the Lord at the time, if I had scripture, I would stand for anything. Brother Wood said that he had received a scripture Amos 4:6. I went up to have Brother Wood lay his hands on me. The next evening, I testified that stains were removed from the front teeth and calcium deposits on the bottom teeth. Even a few, who had not been to the services, commented that I must have recently had them cleaned. Later my dental hygienist commented that my teeth were unusually clean, as per the records I had not been back for a regular cleaning which was long overdue. She told me after I had told her what God had done for me, that not only had He cleaned them for me but she could give witness to the fact. Praise the Lord! Brothers and sisters, trust God! My family and I have not even taken aspirin for over one year. We pray, trust God, believe, wait and receive. Large doses of the Word is our medicine.

Renee Gallier writes:

Brother Gary, when you were at Brother Danny Moye's Church, Agape, in Livingston, Texas, you prayed for me to be delivered from cigarettes. The Lord said, if I would tithe what it would cost me to buy a week's supply of cigarettes that, it would bring deliverance to me. I did that and He gave me a word, that He accepted my sacrifice as a sweet smelling savor in his nostrils. Since then I've had no desire for cigarettes. I can't stand the pitiful smell of them. It has been a long time since I was delivered. I had smoked for 10 years having started when I was 14 years old. PRAISE GOD I'M FREE! Thank you for your prayer. Renee Gallier Frances came to me and gave me $50.00. She wasn't buying a healing but this is what she would have to spend to have a badly decayed tooth fixed. God filled it and removed all her pain.

She was also praying about a pain she had in her left side that was sharp like knife sticking in her. God healed her. She blessed us with this financial offering as an expression of praise for what God did for her.

Janis Hiltibrand writes:

My name is Janis Hiltibrand. I am a member of Church of the Living Water in Deer Park, Texas. On May 6, 1999, I went to church to hear Evangelist Gary Wood. In March, I was laid off from my job of 17 years. I am single and take care of my 73-yearold mother. I was feeling so empty and depressed. The Lord gave

Brother Gary a word for me that my time of mourning was over and to stand on God's promise that He had given to me. Praise God I got a miracle. The next night I received a healing from my precious Lord and Savior. Thank You, Jesus. Brother Gary, through you, Jesus has blessed me more than you will ever know.

HEALED AND FINANCIALLY BLESSED

Dear Brother Gary,

Praise God! Many hearts were touched and stirred to believe God. My heart stirred as you spoke to us and asked us to dance around our billfolds and checkbooks. I received a $300.00 love offering that night. I came to the meeting very sick in my body.

The healing started that night and by Monday I was completely whole.

God Bless,

David Foundry

Van Vleck, Texas

Brother Gary, Everyone was delighted with your testimony. A lady you prayed for was healed of back problems. She had one operation and was scheduled for another one. She now has full movement without pain. The last time I saw her she was playing ball with her boys. Praise God!

Watts Vaughn Sr.

President FGBMFI,

Bay City, Texas

Georgia Whitehead writes:

Thank God for people of God like yourself. The people of the community are still talking about the revival and how the church has grown. You, Deena and Angel were such a blessing to us.

Here is my testimony of God's healing power as He used you to lay hands on me. I had suffered with stomach ulcers and acid reflux. I was taking Prilosec for this condition but it didn't help the discomfort in my stomach. I felt as if I had knots in my intestines.

I was attending a church service in Rockford, Illinois. God gave Brother Gary Wood a Word of Knowledge that someone was having pain in their stomach and it felt like they had knots there.

I knew it was me, but two others came forward for prayer. I got into the prayer line and when you asked me what I wanted the Lord to do for me I said, "It's my stomach, and I'm the one." You prayed and I fell to the floor.

I got up believing I was healed but feeling the same. That night at bedtime, I thanked God for my healing and fell asleep.

Around 2:00 a.m., I woke up and sat in bed. While I was sleeping it felt like someone reached into my stomach and slipped the knots out of my intestines. Before I knew it I said, "I'm HEALED."

I give praise to God from whom all blessings flow through Brother Gary Wood.

Your Sister in Christ,
Evangelist Georgia Whitehead
New Second Baptist Church
Freeport, IL

SHE'S USING THAT NAME

Dear Brother Gary,

In 1981, my husband, Irvin and I were students at the City of Light, Charles and Frances Hunter's Ministry School in Kingwood, Texas. You came and ministered to us regarding your testimony. Your testimony so impacted my life. Later, David Ingles came to the school also and sang the song your miracle inspired him to write, YOU GOT TO GO BACK, SHE'S USING THAT NAME!" It remained in my heart and took deep root.

In 1989, I found my husband dead in the car after coming out of K-Mart where we were shopping. In my frantic actions, I recalled your story and David Ingles' song. Irvin had been dead about an hour. I began CPR and commanded Irvin to come back to me in Jesus' name. In approximately 10 minutes, my daughter Christy said she heard a wind come over her shoulder. She commanded Irvin to begin to breathe and the cardio nurse who had pronounced him dead shouted that he had a pulse. He took a breath and soon we had him STABLE! God spoke to me, that where I would have to walk, I would have to know the power in His name. Your story touched my life in such a powerful way! I have shared it many times.

Joyce Day Winton
Ada, Oklahoma

Kevin Seabough from Jackson, Missouri writes this praise report:

I had poor circulation in my legs from having back surgery. As a result I had very cold feet. After I received prayer and the laying on of hands in Brother Gary's service my feet were warm again.

Gladys Savoy writes:

I first met you at New Covenant Praise Church in Houston, Texas. I went up for prayer for my neck and as you prayed for me you told me I needed a creative healing. I knew that was correct because in 1970 I had an X-ray of my skull done by Dr. Farmer, in Crowley, Louisiana, which showed I was born without a bone in the upper right side of my skull. All that was there was gristle instead of bone.

Pastor DeWitt asked for an elder to stand behind you and me and he prayed for me and all the others who had a need. Later I had an X-ray taken and it showed the space was filled. I no longer have pain there and feel I can hold my head up straight without any discomfort. I am very grateful to you and Pastor DeWitt for your prayers.

Cheslean Sharp writes:

In the summer of 1977, Gary Wood came to visit our prayer troup in Whatron, Texas. Just two days before he came I had suffered a miscarriage. I hadn't told anyone. We had two normal healthy children and I didn't think anyone would understand my heartache. Gary Wood began to prophesy that night as he pointed his finger at me. He said, Sister, God says to dry your tears. He is going to give you another child." I was newly spirit-filled, and had never seen a personal prophecy before. I knew only God knew what happened to me. Gary Wood didn't even know my name and I hadn't been crying at all during the meeting.

Four years later in 1981, my daughter was born. She was followed by two little brothers. I praise God every day for my precious children and I am thankful for His prophet who gave me a "WORD IN DUE SEASON."

Yours in Christ

Cheslean Sharp

Dear Brother Wood,

I would like to thank you for coming to Calvary Temple in Edmond, Oklahoma. I have a wonderful praise report to give.

You remember that you had a special night to pray for our finances. That night we brought our bills to church and you anointed them and prayed over them. I brought a big file box full of bills. I wanted everything prayed for.

It was the night that my husband and I decided to obey the Lord with our tithes. It was hard. After the first two or three times it became easier. Then the Lord spoke to our hearts and said,

"You can't out give Me. Try Me and see what I can do." So we started giving more than we had to spare. Now that was tough, but it was even harder for Isaac to offer up his own son. Back then we were on the verge of bankruptcy. We had a pending law suit against our insurance company for bad faith. It wasn't suppose to settle for another year. Two weeks after you left the suit was settled. We were able to pay off over $13,000.00 in debts. We were able to send a large amount to our missionaries in Old Mexico. We gave $3,000.00 to our own church and we were able to get my husband's car fixed. We now have money in a money market account and don't have to worry which collector is calling next. At the time we started tithing, I was having to work two jobs.

One was very hard for little money. I was able to quit and stay home with my family. I now have money to give to others in need.

Yours in Christ,
Sam and Debbie Drain

THE SPIRIT FLOWS

After Tuesday night service, at the Church of the Living Water in Deer Park, Texas, I went home and opened my mail. I received a notice from the place that holds my student loan. They told me I am receiving a refund of $773.00 off my student loan. Praise God for His care.

MIRACLES AND HEALINGS

A miracle is something that happens instantaneously and the person is made whole. Whatever was wrong with them is healed. If they were blind, they can see; if they were crippled, they can walk; if they were deaf, they can hear; if they were sick, they rise and go about to work. Miracles bring much excitement and glory to God when they happen.

The following biblical examples are clearly stated:

A man who was lame from birth received a miracle when Peter said to him, "Rise and walk in the name of Jesus." Immediately, his feet and ankle bones received strength and he leaped and walked and entered into the temple. [Acts 3:7]

Blind Bartimaeus cried out for Jesus to have mercy on him in Mark 10:47-52. He asked the Lord to restore his sight. Jesus told him that his faith had made him whole and immediately he received his sight and followed Jesus in the way.

In Luke 13:13, Jesus laid his hand on a woman bowed over and said, "Woman, thou art loosed from your infirmity," and immediately she was made straight. Mark 5:29 tells a story of a woman with an issue of blood and she came and touched the hem of Jesus' garment and immediately her issue of blood stopped.

A leper [Luke 5:13] cried to Jesus: If thou wilt thou canst make me clean. Jesus put forth his hand and touched him saying: I will: be thou clean, and immediately the leprosy departed from him. Peter's mother-in-law was sick with a fever. Jesus came and took her by the hand, and lifted her up; and immediately the fever left her, and she ministered unto them.

Healings occur after prayer has been offered and sometimes take time but there is continued improvement in health until perfect health manifests. Jesus did not promise everyone would receive a miracle but he did declare, "They shall recover." [Mark 16:18] A lot of people give up if they don't receive a miracle. They believe God has not heard them. In many cases in the Bible, Jesus waited for faith to come to the sufferers heart and they were willing to do whatever Jesus told them to do. Jesus often said, "According to your faith be it done unto you."

To get faith you need to read the Bible and find God's promises to heal you. This may take time but God's word says in Romans 10:17 that faith comes by hearing and hearing by the word of God.

The Bible says in Ecclesiastes 3:1, to everything there is a season, a time for every purpose under heaven. If you understand that there is a due season it will give you hope and expectancy. Hope is one of the most powerful and energizing words in the English language. Hope gets us up and keeps us going in the hard times, giving us the anticipation of looking toward the future. Hope gives us the reason to live. Hope takes us to faith, which removes the obstacles and changes them to possibilities. Faith does not remove the problem. It changes us.

We can then change the circumstances. Hope, in Greek, indicates an earnest expectation for something about which there is No Doubt At All. Proverbs 10:28 says, The hope of the righteous shall be gladness. It has been said, "A person can live forty days without food, four days without water, four minutes without air, but only four seconds without hope!"

There is no hopeless situation; there are only men and women who have grown hopeless about their situation. When people believe everything will be all right, they become energized and will follow through until victory comes. If people sense defeat, they become tired and give up trying.

Where there is no hope in the future, there is no power in the present.

After the Great Chicago Fire, one businessman hung out this sign in front of his store. "Everything Lost Except: Wife, Children, and Hope. Business will resume tomorrow as usual." Your "due season" will come to you if you will remain faithful and not give up under pressure.

Hebrews 10:23 says, Let us hold fast the profession of our faith without wavering. For he is faithful that promised.

Hebrews 10:35-36 states, Cast not away therefore your confidence, which hath great recompense of reward. For ye have need of patience, that, after ye have done the will of God, ye might receive the promise.

There are Great Rewards for standing on God's Word. The devil, if allowed, does not let you understand this fact, especially when you are under pressure. The enemy's purpose is to shake your confidence in God. Christians should be like 'tea'; our strength should come out when we get into hot water.

The key to coming through and receiving a healing is consistency. You must make up your mind that you will not quit believing just because the healing does not manifest immediately. I once heard Kenneth Hagin say, "If you're willing to stand forever, it will not take very long." If you are willing only to stand for a limited time or you put a time period for the manifestation to happen, then you will be disappointed.

But if you are prepared to stand forever, no matter what the devil throws against you, then you will win.

This attitude is the highest expression of your faith. When there is no evidence in the natural of you being healed or you don't know if it will ever happen, start praising God. Thank Him for His faithfulness even though you don't see the manifestation.

In Mark 4:28 it says, For the earth yields crops by itself; first the blade, then the head, after that the full grain is in the head. The farmer plants the seed and a process called germination starts. The crop does not manifest overnight. It takes time. The farmer's job is to plant the seed and protect it. One day it will come to the time of harvest.

Our daughter is the perfect example of receiving a healing. She was born Angel Marie Wood on November 20, 1971. My wife fell on her stomach during her pregnancy. Angel did not develop properly as she could, and tests from the University of Houston showed she had suffered mental retardation. Doctors and psychologists said she would never achieve over a third grade level of maturity. She also suffered severe allergies that required her to take medication daily.

My wife got an inspired idea and it was for me to read the scripture into a tape recorder and play it in Angel's room at night. We did this and the Word of God began to get inside her spirit. During this time, I was pastoring Full Gospel Fellowship of the Southwest in

Stafford, Texas. There was a retired schoolteacher in our church named Mrs. Headly. She came to me and said God had told her that she could teach Angel to read and write. The school system had given up. She taught Angel to read the Bible. Angel was baptized in the Holy Spirit at an early age. She would speak in tongues and God would give her the answer. We were asked to come to the school once and the teacher asked me what foreign language she was speaking. We got to witness to her about the baptism of the Holy Spirit.

Angel's due season came and now she has her own business and is in the ministry with me, traveling around, giving her testimony and singing. As I wrote earlier in this book, God used her to pray for a woman who called in on KMCT-TV Channel 3 in Monroe, Louisiana.

Some of you have given up because the manifestation has not come immediately. If you understand that there is an appointed time for everything, it will help you not to give up under pressure. In China, there's a plant called the Chinese Bamboo. You plant it and you water it over and over for four years. During that time, you don't see as much as a little sprout. Then, in the fifth year, after five weeks, a little sprout comes forth and it grows ninety feet. There is a due season and if you willing to wait upon the Lord, it will come to pass.

Here are some examples where people had to obey before the miracle took place:

There are recorded incidents in scripture where people had to obey before they received a miracle. In Luke 17:14, some lepers were healed by a miracle as they obeyed Jesus' command to "Go show yourselves unto the priests." In John 9:7, Jesus put clay on a blind man's eyes and told him to wash in the pool of Siloam. It took time for him to go to this pool. He had to grope along until he got there. When he got to the pool and washed, his eyes were opened and he returned seeing. You know, in the natural, this seems very foolish. But obedience creates an atmosphere for miracles.

One time, I accidentally burned my eyes very severely. I should have gone to the doctor, but I just stayed home and my wife prayed for me and put medicine in my eyes. We lived next door to a wonderful family called the Jessups.

Tina and Dana traveled with us around the Houston area and sang songs they had written. Some of those songs were inspired by sermons I had preached. Their mother Mary Ann and the two girls came over to my house to pray for me. I could not see them, and as they walked into my bedroom, I heard a sound like someone was spitting. The I heard Mary Ann's voice say, "Gary, this is Mary Ann." (In John 9, Jesus spit on the ground and then took the spittle and put it in the blind man's eyes. He then told him to go to the pool of Siloam and wash.) "Gary," Mary Ann said. "We have gotten dirt out of the flower garden in your yard, put it in a cup, and we have allowed people that love you to spit into this cup. This is love spittle."

You cannot imagine what I was thinking at this time. Then the unbelievable happened while the girls were singing, Mary Ann slopped that mud into my eyes. For the first time, I knew how that blind man must have felt. As Mary Ann and the girls left, she said, "Go wash at the Pool of Siloam."

I said, "We don't have a Pool of Siloam." She said, "The bathroom, son, the bathroom." As I obeyed these seemingly ridiculous instructions, the minute I put water on my face to wash off the mud and spittle, the burning stopped and my eyes were healed.

The prophet told Naaman who had leprosy to wash in the Jordan River. The Jordan River is very muddy. Naaman came from a land where rivers were very beautiful, and he did not want to obey what the prophet had told him to do. He wanted the prophet to lay hands on him and pray ceremoniously. The word from the prophet to Naaman was to Go dip in the Jordan River seven times, and thou shalt be cleansed from thy leprosy.

MIRACLES AND HEALINGS

When Naaman obeyed, his flesh came again like the flesh of a little child, and he was clean. [2 Kings 5:12-14] GOD EXPECTS OBEDIENCE; MIRACLES ARE INSTANTANEOUS AND HEALINGS TAKE TIME.

WHY SOME ARE NOT HEALED

It is God's will for everyone to healed, the same as it is God's will for everyone to be saved. [2 Peter 3:9; Matthew 18:14] Yet all are not saved, and neither are all healed. You must understand that salvation and healing have two parts: God's part and our part. In Jesus Christ, God provided the sacrifice for our sins and for our healing. He healed all that were sick. That it might be fulfilled which was spoken by Isaiah the prophet saying Himself took our infirmities, and bore our sicknesses. [Matthew 8:16-17] The Biblesays in Isaiah 53:4-5, Surely he hath borne our griefs and carried our sorrows... and with his stripes we are healed. The words borne and carried mean: absolute removal of something from one given place to another.

In the Old Testament, the priest laid his hands on a goat, and it symbolized the transference of their sins to that goat. It was called a Scapegoat. They believed their sins were gone when the Scapegoat died. At Calvary, when Jesus cried, "It is finished," He became our burden bearer. At that moment DEATH AND DISEASE LOST ITS POWER!

Next is OUR PART and that is to ACCEPT or REJECT what God has already provided.

There are reasons why people aren't healed:

A) SIN

God never said He came to heal sinners so they could sin better!

In John 5:14, after Jesus had healed a man, He said unto him: Sin no more, lest a worse thing come upon thee. God has not changed, and He still commands holiness. Sins such as unforgiveness, a critical spirit, murmuring and complaining, and idolatry can stop miracles and healings from taking place in your life. Some folks are involved in the occult and pornography. There are others who have an addiction to ungodly music. All these things are an abomination unto God and we must not have them in our lives.

B) AN UNFORGIVING SPIRIT

Jesus said in Mark 11:25-26, And when ye stand praying forgive, if ye have ought against any; that your Father also that is in heaven may forgive you your trespasses. But, if ye forgive not, neither will you Father which is in heaven forgive you your trespasses. Psalms 66:18 says, If I regard iniquity in my heart, the Lord will not hear me. Faith works by love not hate. [Galatians 5:6]

C) FRIENDSHIP WITH THE WORLD

Ye fight and war, yet ye have not, because ye ask not. Ye ask, and receive not, because ye ask amiss, that ye may consume it upon your lusts. The scripture goes on to say, know ye not that the friendship of the world is enmity with God? Whosoever therefore will be a friend of the world, is the enemy of God. [James 4:2-4] As long as we act like the world, talk like the world, and work for the same purposes as the world, we are enemies of God.

D) LACK OF REAL DESIRE

Some don't want to be healed because they would have to give up the money they get and stop being pampered by those around the house. Until one really wants healing, God will never heal them!

E) UNBELIEF

Jesus could do no mighty miracles in Nazareth because of their unbelief. [Mark 6:5]

F) LACK OF FAITH IN GOD'S WORD

Many treat God's Word just an ordinary book, instead of realizing that with every word they read, God is speaking to them.

G) QUENCHING THE SPIRIT OF GOD

God the Father wills healing. Jesus Christ, the Son of God paid for it at Calvary. The Holy Spirit brings the anointing. The Bible says in Romans 8:11, if the Spirit of him that raised Jesus from the dead dwells in you, he that raised Christ from the dead shall also quicken your mortal bodies by his Spirit. It was the Spirit of God that anointed Jesus to perform all His mighty works: healing the sick and casting out devils. [Luke 4:18] God gave the

Spirit to the Church so that believers could do the same things Jesus did. When the Spirit of God is dwelling in your mortal body, it quickens (gives life) to your physical body.

H) TRADITIONS OF MEN

Some have greater faith in what someone tells them than they do in God's Word. Jesus said, Howbeit in vain do they worship me, teaching as doctrines, the commandments of men... Ye reject the commandment of God, that ye may keep your own traditions... Making the word of God of none effect through your traditions.

[Mark 7:5-13]

Here are some examples of the traditions that bind, versus the truth that sets us free:

(a) Praying "If it be Thy will."

Many have been taught to use the phrase "If it be Thy will" during prayer. Jesus never prayed that kind of prayer concerning sick people. He prayed it as He faced the agony of the cross. He submitted His own will and prayed, "Nevertheless, not My will, but Thine be done." When we pray, "if it be Thy will," it indicates that we do not know exactly what God's will is concerning the things we are praying for. Until you know the will of God concerning a matter, you cannot pray with FAITH, and without FAITH it is impossible to please God.

[Hebrews 11:6] God expects us to know exactly what His will is concerning the things we are praying for.

This is why many sick people don't receive their healing—because they do not know enough of God's Word to be convinced that it is God's Will to heal them. Everything we get from God comes because we believe His Word and accept what is offered.

(b) Saying, "My Sickness Is For The Glory Of God."

God is not glorified when you are sick, any more than He is when you are living in sin! You GRIEVE God when you are sick, and will not receive what He has suffered to give you!

(c) Asking, "If Thou wilt."

In Luke 5:12, a leper came to Jesus, uncertain of his right to be healed, and said, If thou wilt, thou canst make me clean. In verse 13, Jesus immediately showed His willingness to heal all—because He never turned anyone away sick!

(d) Saying, "If Thou canst."

A man came to Jesus with his deaf and dumb son, who was terribly afflicted, and said, If thou canst do anything, have compassion on us and help us. He was not certain that God could help him, but saw that others had been helped, so he came asking:

If thou canst do anything... help us. Jesus answered, If thou canst believe, all things are possible to him that believeth. [Mark 9:22-23]

Jesus did nothing for the son until after the father was convinced that God is both willing and able to do what they needed. To receive a miracle or healing you must turn all the Ifs into the positive knowledge that God will and can do what we ask of Him. The more you read God's Word, the more faith you will have.

(e) Many people are not healed because their faith in the doctrines and reasoning of men, is greater than their confidence in God's Word.

I) TRADITIONS THAT BIND

Man says: "The days of miracles are past."

God says: I am the Lord, the God of all flesh; is there anything too hard for me. [Jeremiah 32:27] There never was a day of miracles, but there is a God of miracles.

Man says: "God takes pleasure in afflicting the saints."

God says: I will take sickness away from the midst of thee. [Exodus 23:25] I am the Lord thy God that healeth thee. [Exodus 15:26]

Man says: "God sends sickness on those that obey God."

God says: Satan has bound her. [Luke 13:16]

Man says: "Paul had weak eyes because God had struck him down."

God says: He sent Ananias to pray for Paul. Jesus... hath sent me, that thou might receive thy sight... and immediately there fell from his eyes, as if it had been scales; and he received sight forthwith... [Acts 9:17-18]

Man says: "You must pray first to see if it is God's will to heal you."

God says: Come boldly unto the throne of Grace, that ye might obtain mercy and find grace to help in time of need. [Hebrews 4:16]

Man says: "We cannot know the will of God."

God says: Being filled with the Knowledge of His Will. [Colossians 1:9]

Man says: "Only the disciples had the power to lay hands on the sick, to open blind eyes, and make the lame walk."

God says: These signs shall follow them that believe... [Mark 16:17] The promise of power to do miracles is unto you, and to your children, and to all that are afar off, even as many as the Lord our God shall call. [Acts 2:39]

Man says: "Some are sick for the glory of God."

God says: The multitudes wondered when they saw the dumb to speak, the maimed to be whole, the lame to walk, and the blind to see, and they glorified the God of Israel. [Matthew 15:31] In the Bible, people always glorified God when folks were healed, not while they were tormented by the devil.

Man says: "By my sickness, my family will be brought to God."

God says: Healings bring people to God. And Peter found a certain man named Aeneas, which had kept his bed eight years, and was sick of the palsy. And Peter said unto him: Aeneas, Jesus Christ maketh thee whole, arise and make thy bed. And he arose immediately. And all those that dwelt at Lydda and Sharon saw him and turned to the Lord. [Acts 9:33-36] No one was saved for eight years, but when Aeneas was healed, everybody in two towns were saved!

Man says: "Not all can have the faith that will receive things from God."

God says: Thou meetest him that rejoiceth and worketh righteousness. [Isaiah 64:5] To go to heaven, we have to be made in right standing with God. If thou canst believe, all things are possible. The healing of our bodies is a gift of God offered to us on the same basis as salvation, and is to be accepted by faith. GOD IS

A GOOD GOD AND HE WANTS YOU WELL!

RECEIVE YOUR MIRACLE

No situation is hopeless. No problem is too big that God cannot handle it. In Mark 5, the Bible tells the story of a woman whom for twelve years had been sick with an issue of blood. She had been hemorrhaging all that time, and I'm sure it drained her strength as well as her faith. She had been to doctor after doctor, and found no relief. In Biblical times, they did not have all the modern hospitals, medical supplies, and medicines that we have today. She had spent all the money she had and nothing had changed. She had done everything she knew to do but nothing she did seemed to be right.

Does that describe you? Maybe you are doing everything you know to do and yet the problem seems worse. You may feel like this woman—that there is no hope for you. There is hope for you in Jesus.

There is no condition that Jesus cannot turn around. He is ready to touch you. His power is here to heal you. There is no need He cannot meet.

The doctor does not have the final word. The banker does not have the final word. The judge does not have the final word. Our enemies do not have the final word. Our God has the final word. Believe His Word!

I know well how she felt. On June 8, 1998, the devil launched a heavy attack against me personally and against our ministry. It manifested in many attacks which I believe were aimed at stopping the publication of my book, A Place Called Heaven.

I spent over 33 days in the hospital, including much time in the emergency room, because I was in severe pain. I went through a battery of tests for everything the doctors thought could be wrong. My wife had to get a job during this time because I could not function due to the extreme pain. I had to cancel meetings and undergo an extensive evaluation including: a CT scan, barium enemas, and a colonoscopy.

Now, let me say that during this time, I prayed, read my Bible, and watched my confessions, but the attack continued against me. During this time, I learned that the attack was not against me personally, but against the anointing upon my life.

The devil hates the anointing that flows out of our lives. It destroys him.

In December, my wife's grandmother died. Just before I was to preach at her funeral, a sharp searing pain hit me in the lower right side of the colon, buckling my knees. I prayed, "Oh Jesus, please allow me to finish this service." After the funeral, later that evening, my wife called home to retrieve messages off our answering machine. There were four calls—two from my doctor, and two from a surgeon in Houston. When I reached the doctor, he said I needed to come to Houston immediately.

When we went to the doctor's office, he gave us very disturbing news. He said I had a large cancerous tumor on my colon, and I had Crohn's Disease, which was medically incurable. Also, there were polyps in the bowel, cysts on my liver, and diverticulitis. He said I needed surgery to remove the tumor. Then we could talk about the future direction of my treatment.

I was in severe pain. Many days I was unable to sleep because of the pain. The doctors prescribed 325 mg. of Oxycodene. I was to take one tablet every six hours. I took three just to get some relief. This is a very powerful drug, and later I was told that many Hollywood stars and other have become addicted to it. The next step would be to give me morphine. We left the hospital, and I arrived home dazed to say the least. I turned on TBN and Pastor John Hagee's program was coming on. When he announced the title of his message, faith leaped into my heart, and I knew it was a divine appointment. His message was entitled "Biblical Principles to Cure Cancer." He talked about how FEAR would attack you and how to stand no matter what the doctor's report was. After the doctor gave me the bad report, he said, "But

Mr. Wood, I am not God." I said, "That's the most truthful statement I've heard in the last few months." I told him that I had talked to God that morning and God did not sound like him.

That night, my pastor Curry Juneau and a good friend John Clark, who is an elder in our church, came to our home to pray for me. My pastor prayed as our covering and asked God to baffle the doctors.

The next morning, we went to the hospital very early in the morning. As we were driving to the hospital, my wife and daughter prayed a very powerful prayer for me. I got out of the car. As I walked to the hospital in darkness, I threw up my hands and said, "Jesus, I have laid hands on thousands of people without exaggeration. I have seen you heal every manner of sickness and disease. You said you would satisfy me and give me a long life. I am not satisfied and I have not lived a long life so I'm asking you for a MIRACLE." I was as desperate as the little woman in Mark 5.

I went into the hospital and they began to prepare me for surgery. The surgeon and five other doctors came into the room, and the surgeon asked me what I thought was a strange question.

After telling me that he had looked at the X-rays and report, he asked me why I thought I was there. I said, "Well, you called me while I was out of town and told me to come back to Houston immediately. After I arrived and met with you, you told me that I had a tumor that had to be removed, that I had Crohn's Disease and diverticulitis." I then added that I had received prayer and believed that I was healed. He said, "Well, it looks like you got a grip on this so let's do the surgery." I went into surgery. They gave me a drug that they said would produce anesthesia and put me to sleep. They said I would be in no pain through this procedure. I'm not sure why, but the medication did not work and I was awake the whole time. It as very painful and I prayed in tongues and screamed out the name of Jesus over and over again. The doctors kept patting me on the shoulder saying, "It is going to be all right." They searched for the tumor for 30 minutes and did the procedure three times. Finally, one doctor said to the one doing the procedure, "Are you going to do the biopsy and remove the tumor or not?" The other doctor replied, "On what? On what?"

He said, "Stop the surgery; get everything out of Mr. Wood; let's relieve him of his suffering and take him back to recovery. The tumor is not there." The doctors went and told my wife that the tumor was gone, but they wanted to run further tests on me.

They asked me to stay the night and ran further tests to find the tumor.

The next day, Jo Ann Dupree, my nurse, was in the room with the doctors, and heard them talking about me. She told them that I was her patient, and was wondering what was going on. She asked, "Does he have any inflammation?" The doctor said, "No." She asked, "Does he have any infection?" The doctor said, "No, no it's all gone!" The surgeon, Treneth Baker, called us in and said, "Mr. Wood, I saw the tumor and so did the gastroenterologist on the X-ray." I said, "Yes sir, so did my wife and I." He said, "We had evidence that this inflammatory mass was Crohn's Disease. It's gone!" he said. I thanked him and told him I believed in doctors, but I knew God had healed me. He wrote me an official medical report. It stated that THE INFLAMMATORY MASS WAS NO LONGER PRESENT. We left the hospital, and when I got into the parking lot, I yelled, "I GOT A MIRACLE!"

Now back to Mark 5 and the woman with the issue of blood. As Jesus passed by, this woman made up her mind to touch Him. She began to move towards Jesus in faith. There was a multitude of people pressing around Jesus. It would have been very easy for her to be discouraged and go back home. She had an excuse to quit and just wait until she died. But she refused to give up and you must not either.

She said, "If I can only touch the hem of His garment." She pushed her way closer and closer until she grabbed hold of the Kraspedon on His prayer shawl. When she took hold of that tassel that contained the names of God, one being Jehovah, the Lord our Healer, the Power of God was sent through her body and she was healed. In the Greek, it states that Jesus said, "Who grabbed me?

Who took hold of me until the power of God went out of me into them? Who grabbed My healing power?" This kind of desperate act gets God's attention. When you come to the end of yourself, and you let God move on your behalf, He will. Do you realize that for you to live a life that is peaceful, you must come to a place where you fully surrender? He wants us to give Him all our cares and burdens. He is stronger than we are. Jesus wants you to be totally dependent upon Him. He said, without me you can DO NOTHING. If you will lose yourself, you will gain Him.

This woman came before Jesus trembling. For years, she had been ostracized by society. She was fearful because she knew she had broken the law. She reached out in a crowd of people and touched somebody, and it was forbidden by the law. Her faith gave her courage to reach out to Jesus.

When the law says you cannot, faith says you can. Faith gives you the confidence to believe God. She started to do what she was had been forbidden. She dared to do what the law said she could not. She knew the penalty. She could have been stoned for doing what she did, so she came before Jesus trembling.

Jesus called her forth because He was going to do something special for her that day. He called her, "Daughter." He knew her physical body had been healed, but He put her back into society whole. Now she had a home, and would not have to worry anymore about what society was going to say about her because Jesus had healed her body, and restored her as a child of God. Her healing was complete, from the crown of her head to the soles of her feet.

God wants you well. He wants healing in your physical body, and in your mind as well. Right now, see Jesus walking by wherever you are. As He comes into your room, reach out and grab hold of Him. Take your eyes off your circumstances, and focus totally on Jesus.

The power of God is flowing towards you like a mighty river. God is present whenever you are ready to allow Him to meet your greatest need.

Lord Jesus, I come against every power of Satan and his demonic forces. I come against any affliction Satan has put upon people reading this book. Jesus, I believe

You came to destroy every work of the devil. I pray for every work of Satan to be destroyed in Jesus' name. I plead the blood of Jesus and release healing power to meet every need. Lord, we grab hold of it. We claim it right now in Jesus' name, and we thank You for it.

Amen.

TESTIMONIES

Praise God. Jesus breaks every fetter and sets us free. Believing there is a Heaven to gain this former addict writes:

Dear Gary:
Your book changed my life. I've read a lot of books, but nothing like yours. I've been a cocaine addict for 20 years. The real message everybody needs to hear is in your book. It's incredible. There is not way you could make this up. Everything you say is in the Bible.

The demons were real in my life. After reading your book, I went to a treatment program. I have decided to follow Christ. I have been baptized and am attending a good church. Recently, I had an opportunity to share with our youth gropu what drugs can do to a person. I believe everyone should read your book.

Mark Blevins,
Las Cruces, New Mexico

Miracles

Dear Gary & Family,

I pray for you, Gary. I know that you are traveling and working hard at preaching the gospel and getting people saved and filled with the Holy Ghost.

Bless you, my Brother,

Rey Lira,

Friendswood, Texas

Dear Gary,

Greetings from Andrews, Texas. I saw you in Odessa in 1980 at a Full Gospel Business Men's Fellowship. Also you came to Andrews Christian Center in the 1980s. Since then I've seen you 3 or 4 times on KMLM. What a great blessing you always are. I marvel every time I see and hear you, Angel, and your precious family.

Leia Forbes

Andrews, Texas

Dear Angel,

Oh, how you blessed me. I am so thrilled to have your book. I am blessed. God bless.

Alma Umber

Ada, Oklahoma

TESTIMONIES

Dear Gary, Deena & Angel,

We wanted to tell you that the Lord has blessed our church so much financially since you were here that we paid our church of and are debt free. We are praising God! We are sending a check as seed faith into your ministry. We love you all.

Pastor Johnny & Jean Seabaugh

Good News Christian Center

Jackson, Missouri

Dear Gary,

Thanks for sending us your book and encouraging us. We will certainly lift our prayer requests to God for a baby the way you taught us to. When you come back to Singapore next year, we want you to share in our church. You have been a blessing to us. May the Lord continue to watch over you.

Edward and Geralidine

Heng Singapore

To Gary and Deena Wood,

Thank you for all the books. I pray these books will touch the lives of my loved ones and friends who are not saved. May God continue to bless you and your work.

Katie Franco

Singapore

Miracles

Dear Gary & Deena,

It was so nice of you to return my call right away. I am hoping and trusting for some new "souls" for that wonderful place called heaven. I can tell you, I read your book to my husband, as we were driving to Tennessee to go to my brother's funeral. I read the different things you were shown in heaven as we were going to his funeral. He was definitely living for Jesus and ready to go to you, Lord Jesus.

Love in Christ,

Mrs. Faye Lee

Sharewood, Illinois

Dear Gary,

In 1981, I had a neighbor whose small son would to go church with me. He would ask me to pray for his mother to be saved. She wasn't very sociable. You can imagine my surprise when she called me early one morning just bubbling. She talked for two hours telling me she had been born again and filled with the Holy Ghost. You were there and gave your testimony. As you were preaching this morning I realized it was you.

Dorothy Bratcher

Kennedale, Texas

Dear Gary & Family,

I was so blessed by your ministry here. This has been a really rough year, and I really needed the encouragement. We pray that your ministry will continue to increase and be a blessing to those around you. Thank you again for sharing so much with us while you were here. We really look forward to having you come again to our church. God bless you greatly. We love you.

Phyllis Miller
Converse, Indiana

To Who It May Concern,

Please receive this as a recommendation of Gary Wood Ministries.

I have personally experienced the anointing that follows this evangelist. Without hesitation, we will have Gary and his family back in our church again! Calvary Temple's senior pastor, Dale Drain, has been acquainted with Gary and family for several years. Throughout this time, Gary has operated in an Evangelistic ministry of God's power. Preaching the word with signs following and most importantly, with integrity. We believe he has a special anointing on his life to do the works of the Lord!

Gary Wood Ministries seem to be in demand with churches and pastors everywhere. We hear testimonies of the power in their meetings, time and again. If you believe God still moves by His Spirit, believe that He is moving through Gary Wood's ministry. You and your congregation will be thoroughly blessed!

In the Service of the Lord,

Rev. David L. Tompkins

Associate Pastor, Calvary Temple

Edmond, Oklahoma

Hi, Mr. Gary Wood,

I am from Singapore. I attend Calvary Charismatic center that is now changed to Victory Family Center. I have read your book A Place Called Heaven that was lent to me from my church sister. Reading your book has blessed my soul so much. I want to share your story with my friends & relatives who are not saved.

I could not find it in any of our bookstores, this is why I am writing to you, to find out how I can order your book. I would like 10 copies of it. Please provide information on the total cost and method of payment. Please reply.

Thank you and God Bless You,

Katie Franco

TESTIMONIES

Dear Brother Wood,

Your testimony was so anointed that the Holy Ghost fell in my living room while I was ironing! I was inspired to go to a higher plane. I planned to give up teaching children's church, but now, I am refreshed and renewed. My determination is to go on with Christ. I am 62 years old and love the Lord. Oh, what a sorrow it would have been for me to give up. Thank you for your testimony and the uplifting words of your beautiful wife and daughter.

Doris King
Colorado City, Texas

Dear Gary,

Hearing your testimony at Church On the Move in Austin blessed me so much. You just don't know what a gift and inspiration your testimony is to the church worldwide.

ANGEL: Just being in the service and hearing your testimony blessed me more than words can describe. Hearing you sing "He's Still Working in Me" made me know God has done wonderful things for you. Your testimony encourages the whole body of Christ.

In Christ,
Rachel Young
Austin, Texas

Financial Miracle

I am a member of the Church of The Living Water. On May 6, I went to church to hear you. In March, I was laid off my job of 17 years! I am single and take care of my 73 year old mother. I was feeling so empty and depressed. The Lord gave you a word for me that my time of mourning was over, to stand on God's promise until I got a miracle. Praise God, the next night I received a healing from my precious Lord. Thank you, Jesus.

God bless you and your family,

Janis Hiltibrand

Deer Park, Texas

The Spirit Flows

Gary,

You invited someone to come that was suffering a tailbone accident. I felt the Spirit move me and I took the leap of faith to believe for my healing. I got instant relief of my lower back pain.

Thank the Lord for Gary's journey to A Place Called Heaven!

Love and blessings to you and your family,

Carlos, Lisa, Kristy Ybarra

Deer Park, Texas

Dear Brother Gary,

Just a note to tell you how much we love and appreciate your and your powerful ministry. Our men's retreat this past weekend was awesome. We believe that resistance in the Spirit was broken during revival the week before. We also believe many things were accomplished for the Lord. Lives were changed in those short two weeks. Thank you for standing with me for the complete healing as was spoken through you by the Lord. I hope this gift for your computer will enable you to reach the harvest for Jesus.

In His love,

Larry & Leila Ewert

Deer Park, Texas

Brother and Sister Wood,

I heard you during the revival at Evangelistic Temple in Ada, Oklahoma. The Lord has a wonderful work to do through you. May you be richly blessed.

Cindy Shaffer

Brother Gary,

Everyone was delighted with your testimony. A lady you prayed for was healed of back problems. She had one operation and was scheduled for another one. She now has full movement without pain. The last time I saw her, she was playing ball with her boys.

Praise God!

Watts Vaughn Sr.

President FGBMFI

Bay City, Texas

Here's another testimony from Shiprock:

Sunday morning all the precious people came to me telling me how much my coming meant to them. Many gave me beautiful turquoise jewelry for my family and myself.

I will never forget all the precious words that were spoken to me. This was the best visit I have ever had on the reservation.

While I was in Shiprock, I was privileged to meet Lucretia Lee who I had prayed for during the camp meeting last year. Her baby was breach and I when I prayed for her, the baby turned over in her womb, and she had no problem from that point on. Up to that time, she could hardly stand up straight. During the service that night, a spirit of laughter came over the church and she was really laughing with holy laughter. The whole place was filled with the joy of the Lord. As a result, she named her baby Isaac, which means laughter. God is so good! We are so happy!

My testimony has been translated into the Navajo language and is now being spread through the Indian nation.

Dear Gary,

I have been a member of Lakewood Church for 23 years. I know when the people receive a speaker. I've heard a lot of good comments about you and your daughter. I was a great message. I felt encouraged and Angel's testimony was so beautiful. That is a miracle itself. I felt like I'd been to church. You were really anointed and I just soaked it up. Your greatest days are ahead of you.

Gladys Pope
Houston, Texas

Dear Brother Gary,

Just a note to tell you thanks for being such a blessing to me last week. You will never know what those cuff links mean to me. They are truly a confirmation and affirmation to me that I am doing exactly what God wants me to do. No one but the Holy Spirit would have known that I needed cuff links and I appreciate your willingness to listen and obey.

God Bless
Dr. Paul Osteen
Lakewood Church
Houston, Texas

I heard you give your testimony at Lakewood and was so blessed. Pray for my mother who's crippled in a nursing home.

Mary Agular
Lubbock, Texas

We were so excited watching Gary's face as he talked about going to Heaven. What a "Blessing" it was. I am so thankful he told everyone about it.

Peggy Lyle Hill
Pleasant Hill, Illinois

Dear Beloved Brother Gary,

Greetings in the name of our Lord Jesus Christ. Thank you for sharing your testimony with the body of Christ. You have had an experience that many of us have only dreamed of. Reading your book allows us to walk through Heaven with you. Thank you so very much.

TESTIMONIES

Your friend and brother in Christ, Randy Thanks for sending our Newsletter. I enjoyed it and like keeping up with what is going on in your ministry.

God Bless each of you,

Jerry & Wanda Tucker

Cisco, Texas

Brother Gary,

When you were at our church, "Open Door Fellowship" in Converse, Indiana, I had a deposit under my kneecap causing me pain and a limp.

You prayed for me helping me to release my faith and expect God to move in my life. Two days later He did. The pain and limp are gone. "Praise the Lord."

Charlie Martin

Open Door Fellowship

Converse, Indiana

Dear Gary Wood,

I enjoyed reading your book on Heaven. It was such a blessing. I am planning on sending your book to a prisoner who has been struggling with alcohol for a long time. Thanks so much.

Betty Auchuker

Friendswood, Texas

Hi Gary,

I finished your book and listened to your tape. I was so blessed. My daughter is reading it now. When you were on Marcus and Joni Lamb's program, I taped it and my sister and her family played it over and over again. Thanks so much.

Carolyn Pingley Beverly,
West Virginia

Dear Gary,

Please send your book as soon as possible because I know it is going to be a blessing to me.

Davis Brown
Bishopville, South Carolina

Mr. Gary Wood,

I have heard your testimony on Channel 29 KMPL. I was very informative. I have never heard that many details of Heaven before.

Macie Duncan
Ft. Worth, Texas

Brother Wood,

Thank you for sending me your book A Place Called Heaven. I received it today and I had to stay up until I finished reading it. I have several people in mind I want to share it with. I heard you years ago at Pastor Fred Hall's church in Tomball. God Bless you and thanks again for the book.

Audrey Allison
Tomball, Texas

I enjoyed seeing you on TV with Joni and Marcus. Blessings to you and your ministry.

Rose Allen
Dallas, Texas

Dear Gary Wood,

I saw you on Celebration with Marcus and Joni Lamb. We enjoyed your testimony very much. God bless you and your ministry.

Yours truly,
Mrs. Joe Smith
Mesquite, Texas

Dear Gary & Deena,

Thank you for the book, video, and Good News. I am still trying to absorb all of this wonderful information. I pray and believe God will continue to grow your ministry.

Deanna Reeve
Mesquite, Texas

Thank you for the book A Place Called Heaven. It is wonderful.

Carol Farcher

Denver, Colorado

Dear Brother Gary,

We certainly appreciate your coming to the church in our absence. We have been announcing it and the people are looking forward to seeing and hearing you again. God continues to bless you and your work for Him.

Sincerely,

Pastor Fred Duncan

Cornerstone Foursquare Church

Houston, Texas

After the homegoing of Tom Shaw of Elisha Ministries, Inc., his wife Teressia wrote us this message. Thanks for the beautiful card. Your book was a real comfort to me.

Teressia Shaw

Elisha Ministries

Madill, Oklahoma

Hi Deena,

Hope this little note finds you and your family happy and well. I really loved Gary's book. I was especially happy to read on page 25, where he wrote that he saw all kinds of animals with the children. I was so nice meeting you and I hope to see you again sometime. God bless you both.

Nancy Beaver

Houston, Texas

Dear Brother Gary and Sister Angel,

Thanks so much for accepting our invitation to be a part of our Sunday morning services. Our schedule looks best for February 20, 2000. What we hope to do is to have Angel share for a couple of minutes, followed by a duet with Dad. We will need to limit the time to no more than five minutes. I know that this will be a tremendous blessing to not only our church, but the television audience as well.

Brother Gary, if you can let me know as soon as you can check your schedule, it would be helpful. I'll get you in touch with our soundman so that you can make arrangements for your music.

God bless, we love you,

Paul Osteen

Dear Mr. Gary Wood,

Greetings from Singapore! First of all, both Edward and myself would like to say a big "Thank You" for praying with us for a baby and teaching us how to pray for one. We are deeply grateful for your constant encouragement in your letters to us. We will be first time parents in early September this year. Praise the Lord! I am now 10 weeks pregnant. We rejoice because this is a much-awaited good news we would like to share with you and we know you will be happy for us too.

Edward & Gerry Singapore

Right now, God wants to save you. He will never turn anyone away. For whosoever shall call upon the name of the Lord shall be saved. [Romans 10:13]

Dear God,
I want to become a born again Christian. I confess I am a sinner. I believe You sent Your Son to die on the cross for my sins. I confess with my mouth that Jesus Christ is Lord. Thank You, Lord, for allowing me to become a part of Your Christian family.
In Jesus' Name I pray, Amen.
A genuine born again Christian wants above everything else to do the will of God. Don't be ashamed to be a witness to others and tell them how to become a Christian. Join a Bible believing church and be baptized in water as an act of faith to let the world know you are following Christ's example.

✳ ✳ ✳

If you would like to receive the Holy Spirit, ask the Father in Jesus' Name to fill you with the Holy Spirit. Believe you receive when you ask and begin to speak your new language in faith as God gives it to you.

Repeat this prayer:

Father,

I come to You in faith believing that Jesus Christ died in my place for my sins and rose from the dead. I ask You to fill me to overflowing with Your Holy Spirit. You said in Your Word that if I asked I would receive, so I ask You now to fill me to overflowing with Your precious Holy Spirit. I receive Him now by faith and expect to speak with other tongues as He gives me the utterance.

In Jesus' Name I pray,

Amen!

✳ ✳ ✳

Now I want to pray for your healing. Put your hand on your body where you are sick and repeat this prayer:

Lord Jesus, You are the Great Physician. All healing comes through You. I speak Your Word over this body and thank You that You heal all our diseases. Thank You for healing and enabling me to walk in health.

In Jesus' Name I pray,

Amen!

TESTIMONIES

To contact Evangelist Gary Wood about ministry or scheduling in your church, please write or call:

Gary Wood Ministries
P.O. Box 1649
Sugarland, TX 77487
281-491-4836
e-mail: garywoodmi@aol.com
www.garywoodministries.com

CPSIA information can be obtained at www.ICGtesting.com
Printed in the USA
LVOW12s1403051213

363909LV00009B/185/P

9 780989 221382